TWENTIETH CENTURY

INTERPRETATIONS

OF

A STREETCAR NAMED DESIRE

TWENTIETH CENTURY INTERPRETATIONS

OF

A STREETCAR NAMED DESIRE

A Collection of Critical Essays

Edited by
JORDAN Y. MILLER

Prentice-Hall, Inc. *Englewood Cliffs, N.J.*

A SPECTRUM BOOK

Acknowledgment is gratefully made to the following publishers for permission to quote from the works of Tennessee Williams:

To New Directions Publishing Corporation and to International Famous Agency for quotations from *A Streetcar Named Desire* (© 1947 by Tennessee Williams) and *27 Wagons Full of Cotton* (© 1945 by Tennessee Williams)

To Random House, Inc., for quotations from *The Glass Menagerie* (© 1945 by Tennessee Williams and Edwina D. Williams)

10 9 8 7 6 5 4 3 2 1

PRENTICE-HALL INTERNATIONAL, INC. (*London*)
PRENTICE-HALL OF AUSTRALIA, PTY. LTD. (*Sydney*)
PRENTICE-HALL OF CANADA, LTD. (*Toronto*)
PRENTICE-HALL OF INDIA PRIVATE LIMITED (*New Delhi*)
PRENTICE-HALL OF JAPAN, INC. (*Tokyo*)

Contents

TWENTIETH CENTURY

INTERPRETATIONS

OF

A STREETCAR NAMED DESIRE

Introduction

by Jordan Y. Miller

I. Brief Biography

During the theater season of 1938–1939, New York's Group Theatre, under Harold Clurman's direction, sponsored a contest for aspiring playwrights under twenty-five. Although only a single prize was contemplated, three one-act sketches collectively entitled *American Blues* so impressed the judges that a special citation and one hundred dollars were tendered to one Thomas Lanier Williams of St. Louis, who said he was born March 26, 1914. Perhaps the subsequent career of this shy, mild young man from the Midwest who spoke with a soft Southern accent depended on it, perhaps not, but that three-year stretch of the truth did bring to the attention of those who mattered at a very propitious moment the name and talents of one whose actual birthdate of March 26, 1911, now hardly matters at all. What followed after the opportune white lie, however, most certainly does.

The marriage of Cornelius Coffin Williams and Edwina Dakin is reminiscent in many ways of the grossly ill-matched union of James O'Neill and Ella Quinlan, parents of the only other American playwright to whom Tennessee Williams can successfully be compared. Eugene O'Neill, too, grew up in a home dominated by a blustering, hard-drinking, parsimonious father whose long stretches on the road made him almost a stranger to his children. In total antithesis was the gentle, sensitive, beautiful mother, raised in a protected religious atmosphere, far removed from her husband in talents and interests. To be sure, the elder Williams, telephone exchange manager and successful shoe salesman, descendant of an old and prominent Tennessee family, had personally little in common with the national matinee idol who rose from the poverty of Irish immigrant stock; and the former Mississippi debutante who provided a loving, understanding refuge for the Williams children had almost as little identification with the unworldly convent graduate eventually to succumb to the relentless grip of drug addiction, so horrifyingly portrayed in O'Neill's *Long Day's Journey Into Night*. Yet one cannot help marking the astonishing likeness of the home backgrounds of these two dramatic

1

artists, whose tragic outlook was to have such signal impact upon American stage literature.

Tennessee Williams—the name has never been clearly explained even by Williams himself, although his mother offers speculation that her son somehow identified with early Indian fighters among his Tennessee ancestors—was born, first son and second child, into the Episcopal rectory home of his maternal grandparents, The Rev. and Mrs. Walter E. Dakin, in Columbus, Mississippi, although, as Mrs. Williams corrects the common story, the birth was in a small local hospital instead of the rectory itself. With the father frequently absent and expressing very little interest in or understanding of his son whenever he was home, the strong influences on the first seven years of Williams' life came from the sheltering mother, the kindly grandparents, and the devoted sister, Rose, two years his elder, as well as from the black nursemaid, Ozzie. Some say that young Tom was early witness to the darker, even seamier sides of human nature while accompanying his grandfather on parish visits, encountering death and suffering at a highly impressionable age. Perhaps, although the evidence is not substantial. On the other hand, he personally recalls even now the wild and chilling tales told by Ozzie, but she departed the family when Williams was only six. There is no doubt at all, however, but that his extremely close relationship with his beautiful, imaginative, highly impressionable sister became of tremendous importance. In their near-idyllic years in Columbus and Clarksburg, Mississippi, and in Nashville, they invented endless games, passing days, months, and years of memorable childhood pleasure. Her twofold loss profoundly affected Williams, both as a child and as an adult artist. First, her abrupt entrance into womanhood, an act of nature that neither could understand, removing Rose almost overnight from their closed children's world, was a trauma to them both, later to be beautifully described in "The Resemblance Between a Violin Case and a Coffin." Then, over the years, a slow regression into schizophrenia ended in a suspended half-life existence following a prefrontal lobotomy in 1937. This act of surgical violence, so painfully reflected in the central theme of *Suddenly Last Summer,* was done without Williams' knowledge, but he long held himself responsible for its catastrophic consequences.

An attack of diphtheria at the age of five left the formerly active child a virtual cripple for about two years. Williams disputes his mother's assertion that his legs were paralyzed, although it seems very clear that he was left severely weakened and all the more dependent upon his sister. Then, hardly recovered, he was moved with the family in the heat of the summer of 1918 to St. Louis, where Cornelius Williams had been promoted to a desk job with the International Shoe

Company. Scarcely seven years old, Tom Williams found his pleasant Southern life permanently at an end. With his father more and more at home, totally alienated from the delicate child whom he ridiculed as "Miss Nancy" and shouting about the house in a voice "sometimes like thunder," Williams found no replacement in a succession of city apartments for the easy rural and suburban living that he had known during the years with his maternal grandparents.

A year's respite with the Dakins in Clarksburg during his mother's recovery from influenza in 1919 after the birth of her second son, Dakin, enabled Williams to lose himself in his grandfather's library of Dickens, Scott, and Shakespeare. Not long after his return to St. Louis he began to write, and at the age of eleven his mother delighted him with the gift of a battered secondhand typewriter on which he clattered out endless pieces. Soon writing became a form of escape, a comforting refuge from a home life regarded as increasingly sordid. By the time he was fourteen he had seen some short poems printed in a school paper, and in 1927, at the sophisticated age of sixteen, his professional career got underway with a five-dollar check from *Smart Set* magazine for an essay on the subject "Can a Good Wife Be a Good Sport?" He thought not. Then in June 1928 *Weird Tales* published his "The Vengeance of Nitocris," accompanied by payment of thirty-five dollars. In this account, the horrible revenge of an Egyptian queen who drowned her revelling guests reflected the young writer's attraction to a kind of gratuitous violence that had fascinated him (as he admits) in such plays as Shakespeare's *Titus Andronicus*.

Williams entered the University of Missouri in the fall of 1929. He turned completely collegiate, joined a fraternity, discovered that alcohol relieved his acute shyness, and made the wrestling team. His father, proud veteran of the Spanish-American War, was enraged when young Tom failed ROTC. This was the last straw for a parent so completely blind to the significance of his son's abilities in writing that he saw them only as degrading and effeminate, and he abruptly pulled the boy out of school a year short of graduation and placed him in the stockroom of the shoe company. Williams had already suffered humiliation at the hands of his father in the separation from his high school sweetheart, one Hazel Kramer, whose parents had been persuaded to send her to a different college. Now, this same parental interference had placed him in a job in which he suffered a daily "living death." Compensation came only at night when, armed with coffee and cigarettes, he remained in his room at home where he wrote and wrote, sometimes collapsing fully clothed on the bed, where he would be found by his mother the next morning.

Although he had entirely recovered from the childhood attack of diphtheria, Williams was constantly aware of his physical handicaps, including a growing blindness in one eye caused by a cataract which was never successfully removed despite four operations. His tendencies toward hypochondria and a conviction that he would die of a heart attack quite suddenly at any time can probably be dated from the Sunday in March 1935 when he and Rose were returning from a movie. Stricken by violent palpitations, he was rushed by his sister to a hospital, where his trouble was diagnosed as complete exhaustion. Whether it was a mild stroke or a mild breakdown, the attack ended his work at the shoe company. During recovery in Memphis at the home of his retired grandfather he wrote and saw produced for the first time one of his own plays, a farce entitled *Cairo! Shanghai! Bombay!* presented on July 12, 1935, by a local theatre group called the Garden Players.

In 1936, with tuition provided by his grandmother, Williams entered Washington University in St. Louis and more of his plays began to see production. First, the Theatre Guild of suburban Webster Groves presented *The Magic Tower.* Then he joined The Mummers, a small Bohemian group of students and poets, for whom he wrote a curtain-raiser called *Headlines* for their production of Irwin Shaw's anti-war drama *Bury the Dead.* This was followed by *Candles in the Sun,* a highly melodramatic story of coal miners, about whom Williams knew absolutely nothing. *Me, Vashya!,* concerning a munitions maker in World War I, was submitted in a Washington University contest but failed to win a prize. The author took strong issue with the verdict in the form of a somewhat more than indiscreet letter to the Dean, the first display of his subsequent tendency to react with acute displeasure to negative critical opinion of his work. In 1937, with tuition once more from his grandmother, he enrolled at the University of Iowa. In addition to *The Fugitive Kind,* which The Mummers produced in 1938, he also wrote a play "very specifically" about love called *Spring Storm* and a rather harrowing prison play, *Not About Nightingales.*

Williams received his A.B. degree from Iowa in 1938, and almost immediately he embarked upon a life that, save for periods in or near New York during the mounting of a new play, became almost totally peripatetic. He felt he could no longer remain in St. Louis. As he watched his parents grow more and more estranged (total separation occurred in 1947) and his sister become lost to him behind the walls of mental institutions, he felt increasingly adrift. During the summer of 1938 he attempted without success to join the Chicago WPA Writers' Project, then returned briefly to St. Louis, to depart almost immediately thereafter, for no apparent strong reason, for New Orleans. Failing to enter the WPA Writers' Project in that city as well, he headed for the Southwest and California, where jobs in a shoe store and on a pigeon ranch kept him alive. While living in Culver City, California, he received notice of the special citation from the Group Theatre for *American Blues,* accompanied by its hundred-dollar check. There followed a chain of events in which Williams established his long and very successful relationship with Audrey Wood who, as his exclusive agent, immediately sold his "A Field of Blue Children" to *Story Magazine.* It was the first published work to carry the name of Tennessee Williams.

Using the hundred-dollar prize money to support himself at Laguna Beach in the summer of 1939, Williams worked on a play he was to call *Battle of Angels.* When the money ran out he journeyed to New York to find a job, but failure there resulted in a brief return to St. Louis. Then a telephone call from Miss Wood in December of 1939 announced a Rockefeller grant of $1,000, which would enable him to work seriously on his writing. He returned to New York, where John Gassner, teaching playwriting at the New School, hailed *Battle of Angels* as one of the best new scripts he had seen in some time. The Theatre Guild took an option on the play, but without notifying them of his whereabouts, Williams took the last of his grant money supplemented by a few Guild option checks, and went to Mexico for rest and further writing. He was completely surprised, therefore, to learn from a newspaper item in the fall not only that the play was to be produced but that Miriam Hopkins, one of the big names in the theater world, was interested in playing the lead.

Thus the professional career of Tennessee Williams, playwright, began with great promise. It very nearly ended once and for all with the Boston tryout of *Battle of Angels,* one of the genuine disasters of the 1940–1941 season, or any other, for that matter. Even with Margaret Webster directing, the drama of violence and seduction almost suffocated the audience and the critics with its pyrotechnics, including a badly bungled stage-effect fire. "One of the most incredible dramas ever presented in Boston," said one morning reviewer, and the stunned Guild sent its subscribers a letter of apology for the fiasco. Williams retired in confusion to Key West, where he attempted to salvage the play, but it never opened again in anything like its original form.

For the next two years, with a failure of monumental proportions behind him, Williams wandered here and there, living in Georgia, Washington, D.C., Florida, St. Louis, New Orleans, and New York, with income from a small renewal of his Rockefeller grant and odd jobs such as teletype operator and elevator man. In 1943 Miss Wood secured him a position as scenarist at Metro-Goldwyn-Mayer, but he did not last the original six months of the contract, unable to write for Lana Turner and Margaret O'Brien in the manner to which they were accustomed. After staying at Malibu Beach, living on the salary residue from his MGM contract, he submitted another "uncommercial" play, as he termed it, to Miss Wood, originally entitled *The Gentleman Caller*. Deeply moved by it, Miss Wood submitted the script directly to actor-director Eddie Dowling, who accepted it at once. The play became *The Glass Menagerie* and the rest is history.

The Glass Menagerie opened on December 26, 1944, at Chicago's Civic Theatre to uniformly enthusiastic critical reception. It was an instant success in New York the following March 31, when it returned Laurette Taylor to the stage in a triumphant comeback and established Tennessee Williams as a playwright of national importance. It won the New York Critics' Circle Award for 1944–1945, and its box office appeal made Williams affluent beyond his wildest imagination. With income sufficient to enable him to retire to Mexico, Key West, and New Orleans, he worked on other plays, among them one called *The Poker Night*, while his second New York production, *You Touched Me!*, based on a story by D. H. Lawrence, opened in September 1945. It closed, despite excellent performances by another strong cast, after lukewarm notices and a few months' run, but it was a clear tribute to Lawrence, whom Williams greatly admired, and whose literary themes and viewpoints run throughout a number of his own works. Finally, after having molded *The Poker Night* into *A Streetcar Named Desire*, he sent it off to Miss Wood who, once again immediately enthusiastic, secured Irene Selznick to produce it and Elia Kazan to direct it.

With the December 3, 1947, production of *A Streetcar Named Desire*, Tennessee Williams—slight, shy, now half-blind, an acute hypochondriac, essentially homeless, a most unobtrusive and unprepossessing young man of thirty-six—became a world figure. A second New York Drama Critics' Circle Award and a Pulitzer Prize followed at once, and "O'Neill, Miller, and Williams" soon came to mean the greatest that American drama and theater could offer.

To continue an account of his life beyond this point seems superfluous. Never one to make the headlines, never marrying, an artist dominated by the powerful forces of the tragic spirit, Williams continued to pour forth—from Key West, Mexico, Europe, or wherever—an impressive accumulation of work. Though more versatile than O'Neill had been, departing on occasion into story and verse, he maintained essentially the same tragic view, calling down upon himself much of the praise and much of the condemnation directed at his predecessor a generation earlier. The violence of brutal sex, the hate, the suffering, the frustrations were always there—even the comedies seemed constantly on the "dark" side—but evident, as well, were great compassion and sympathy for those caught in the web of tragic destiny.

But comparisons are misleading, and, in the final analysis, irrelevant. The stamp of Tennessee Williams is distinctively his own, in success and failure alike. Even a selective listing is impressive: *Summer and Smoke,* only modestly successful in 1950, gained a high place in the Williams canon in its Off Broadway production of 1952; the lusty comedy of *The Rose Tattoo,* 1951; the highly stylized hysteria of *Camino Real,* 1953; a third Critics' Circle Award and a second Pulitzer Prize for *Cat on a Hot Tin Roof* in 1955; *Sweet Bird of Youth,* 1959; and yet another Critics' prize for *The Night of the Iguana* in 1961 all combine into a total of substantial proportions. Though a long list of failures since then—*The Milk Train Doesn't Stop Here Anymore* in at least three versions beginning in 1961, *The Seven Descents of Myrtle* in 1968, and *In the Bar of a Tokyo Hotel* in 1969 —has been discouraging, there is constant hope that the "old" Williams will successfully emerge, or that the "new" Williams will some day arrive.

II. *The Place of* Streetcar *in the Postwar Theater*

The last New York season of the 1960s rang down on a grand total of some twenty-one new productions available along what once was called "The Great White Way." Scarcely a dozen new plays, hardly more than half a dozen musicals were contributed to the last year of a decade of steady decline on "Broadway." Exciting things continued to flourish "off" and "off off" the main drag in the lofts, brownstones, and assorted arenas both sides of Greenwich Village, but the big houses that border the honky-tonk obscenity called Times Square continued their steady plod toward obscurity.

To look back, then, at December 3, 1947, the opening night of *A Streetcar Named Desire,* is to look almost wistfully into a past that now seems remotely far away. The billboards of the day proclaim a flourishing postwar American theater of great prosperity and promise. Marquee lights spell the names of long-familiar producers, directors, and actors still performing in an enterprise little changed from what it was after Eugene O'Neill forced it to take itself seriously in the fifteen or twenty years before Pearl Harbor. The theatre-goer not privileged to find out if this play about an odd-sounding trolley is worth the price of an opening-night ticket still has the luxury of twenty-seven other choices. There are Thomas Mitchell in J. B. Priestley's mystical *An Inspector Calls,* and Paul Kelly as the determined general officer of *Command Decision.* Helen Hayes is trying light comedy in *Happy Birthday,* Frank Fay's comeback heads *Harvey*'s six-foot invisible rabbit-philosopher toward one of the longest runs in New York theater history, and Bert Lahr wows them in *Burlesque*. *Born Yesterday*, having launched Judy Holliday to stardom, runs on. Jane Cowl and Henry Daniell perform *The First Mrs. Fraser*, and June Lockhart is enchanting in *For Love or Money*. Wendy Hiller and Basil Rathbone treat Henry James with respect in *The Heiress*, competing successfully with John Van Druten's *The Druid Circle* and *The Voice of the Turtle*, as well as Terence Rattigan's display of British honor and justice, *The Winslow Boy*. Rodgers and Hammerstein continue to "revolutionize" the musical comedy with *Allegro*, together with a revival of *Oklahoma! Brigadoon's* fairy tale village appears and vanishes nightly, leprechauns come and go in *Finian's Rainbow*, and Ethel Merman belts out Irving Berlin's *Annie Get Your Gun*. Maurice Evans is reviving Shaw's *Man and Superman*, Judith Anderson is stunning audiences as Robinson Jeffers' Medea, and Katharine Cornell is Shakespeare's Cleopatra. And Edith Piaf still sings. Most wistful of all, orchestra seats are $4.80 top and the last gallery row is only $1.20.

There were new voices to be heard among these established, familiar names, and they seemed to fit remarkably well within the existing dramatic patterns, while giving promise of future contributions of far more than routine note. Back in 1945 had appeared *The Glass Menagerie* from the same young man who provided this exciting December premiere, and another neophyte, Arthur Miller, had done well with *All My Sons* in January of the season just completed. Not far ahead would come William Inge with his impressive ability to portray the little people of middle America in *Come Back, Little Sheba* of 1950.

Inge, for a few more seasons, maintained the well-established realistic traditions of the art with a series of successfully routine dramas of limited distinction, but as the 1950s wore on his themes and, more important, his style became almost anachronistic. The other two, Williams and Miller, apparently still functioning within the same familiar genre of contemporary realistic dramaturgy, actually bridged the decade of the fifties with two productions of startling impact that, in character, theme, and technique left behind the old ways of Inge and his predecessors and prepared in marked measure for what lay ahead. Ironically, neither author has surpassed nor even equalled *Streetcar* of 1947 nor *Death of a Salesman* of 1950, and both works remain, for all the honors and recognition subsequently tendered their creators, the high points not only of two individual playwriting careers but of a traditional theater very soon to be shattered by the absurdists of the 1950s and the nude/rock musicals and revues of the 1960s. The worlds of Genet, Beckett, Ionesco, Pinter, Albee, or even Leroi Jones are not far removed from that of Williams in *Streetcar* or of Miller in

Salesman as one might assume. Williams, in particular, created in his finest drama a significant transitional play, its original brilliance even now retained without loss in a work as important as any other ever written for the American stage.

Language and character, as well as the plot line along which they move, seem at first to place *Streetcar* squarely in the middle of Inge's type of realism. Here are very ordinary, completely unromanticized, and rather unlovely people, immediately recognizable as members of contemporary society, unvarnished, unpolished, behaving in a wholly "natural" manner. They speak a blunt, straightforward language, with actions to match. They are surrounded by the heat, the noise, and the general contamination of an environment created and maintained by their own kind, and what goes on within that environment has no effect beyond the narrow limits of the world visible upon the stage. The problems of the search for individual happiness and security and the day-to-day conflicts of one person with another are those of an indefinite number of others equally unimportant and undistinguished. Neon lights flash, trains roar by, radios blare, couples fight and make love. The rest of the universe takes little note of them.

But of course there is more. Theatrical stylization is obvious in Williams' use of transparent walls, a "simultaneous stage" of multiple acting areas, and carefully controlled, highly symbolic light and sound. Beyond all that, as Elia Kazan, the play's director, points out, Williams creates a conscious stylized effect in his characters and in the dialogue they speak. The almost hypnotic behavior of Stella, her "narcoticized" existence as Kazan sees it, and the gross animalistic performance of Stanley in his relationship to her and in his battle with Blanche, follow a virtually ritualistic pattern. And Blanche herself has entered from and moves within an unreal world, her own elaborate rituals transcending any "normal" or "realistic" behavior.

Finally, in its most important transitional aspect, its theme, *Streetcar* becomes particularly identified with the artistry of those playwrights who were starting to portray onstage a world hopelessly awry, its human occupants ridiculously absurd creations of a malevolent or totally unconcerned universe. The realist of the past was devoted to the literal and detailed recounting of the world's joys, fears, defeats, and successes. What happened to rational men in a society primarily of their own making concerned the artist more than the motive forces themselves; often socially oriented, the realist frequently made strong cause with those who saw a need for the reform of human behavior. Williams, in *Streetcar*, plays a different game. The struggle of Blanche DuBois is not the struggle of Ibsen's Nora Helmer. The assertion of a woman's right to dignity and respect which drives Nora from her toy home is not the life-and-death combat that Blanche endures. The fundamentals that make the human animal function become, for Williams, the violent and brutal forms of nymphomania, homosexuality, mother-fixation, and satyriasis. Thus the emphasis turns to the struggle itself. Williams' graphic demonstration of it does not employ the mechanical, often comical little people who wander helplessly through the absurdists' disinterested universe, for his are characters of considerable dimension and, as we shall see, tragic stature. There is no ultimate solution, for there is no door for Nora to slam on her way to a better, if uncertain, future. The world of Williams remains as menacing as it is impassive.

The monster tragedies of O'Neill's *Strange Interlude* and *Mourning Becomes Electra* had jolted the American theater between wars into a realization of its serious potential, and O'Neill, above all others, had reacted almost violently against the theatrical traditions of his own day. But by the time *Streetcar* appeared, O'Neill had been all but forgotten. His mystic search for man's place with God had pretty well faded, and each technique that had once seemed so shatteringly revolutionary now seemed to be a mere *tour de force,* incapable of imitation or reuse. At first glance one might affirm that Tennessee Williams, in subject matter, theme, and character, dwelling upon the darker side of human nature trapped in the traumas of sex in all its deviant forms, had simply continued where O'Neill left off. A closer study of *Streetcar* qualifies this judgment. Williams, unlike O'Neill, was not a conscious revolutionary in the usual sense. He was not attempting to move the theatre or its drama into any different patterns, and the appearance of *Streetcar* prompted no reviewer to shout that he "cleaves the skylines of tomorrow," as one critic had done in evaluating O'Neill. The critics could, and did, however, proclaim that here was a writer of great theatrical skill and obvious keen awareness of the monstrous forces within the human psyche who could combine the stage conventions of his day into a shattering exploration of doomed souls driven to the ends of tragic desolation. Twenty years after, *Strange Interlude* and *Mourning Becomes Electra* were historical curiosities. Twenty years after, *Streetcar* remains vivid and playable, an effective exploration of human degradation and tragic aspiration, part of that highly traditional past still apparent in the season from which it emerged, but even more a part of the disturbed, explosive present, in which it remains as relevant as ever.

III. Streetcar *as a Tragedy*

The late Joseph Wood Krutch, Brander Matthews Professor of Dramatic Literature at Columbia University at the time *A Streetcar*

Introduction   11

Named Desire opened in New York, discussed the play with his graduate class in modern drama on the morning after he first saw it. "This,"
he said with conviction, "may be it. This may be the great American
play." One wonders if Professor Krutch, observing the Broadway scene
from his Arizona home, to which he later retired to take up his distinguished career as naturalist, retained this high opinion. It would
not be surprising if he did. Although he long held that tragedy in the
classic sense was not really feasible in the twentieth century, his attitude toward Williams' play would very likely include the possibility
that it comes as close to genuine tragedy as any modern American
drama.

If a single character in contemporary American stage literature approaches the classical Aristotelean tragic figure, it must surely be
Blanche DuBois. Deceptive, dishonest, fraudulent, permanently flawed,
unable to face reality, Blanche is for all that thoroughly capable of
commanding audience compassion, for her struggle and the crushing
defeat she endures have the magnitude of tragedy. The inevitability
of her doom, her refusal to back down in the face of it, and the essential humanity of the forces that drive her to it are the very heart of
tragedy. No matter what evils she may have done, nor what villainies
practiced, she is a human being trapped by the fates, making a human
fight to escape and to survive with some shred of human dignity, in
full recognition of her own fatal human weaknesses and the increasing
absence of hope.

The struggle, of and by itself, is thus entirely worth the making, and
all that has gone before in Blanche's life, involving moral and ethical
judgments, is made irrelevant. Blanche may have fought the initial
skirmishes of her last long battle in questionable, unsavory manner,
and the curses of the gods may have justly rested on her head in consequence. But once aware of the fact that the last battle is indeed at
hand with a clearly identified antagonist, even though both battle
and antagonist may have descended upon her as the inevitable result
of past sins of her own making, she takes her final stand with defiant
courage. Any judgment of her, then, must be made only in terms of
her behavior in the tragic protagonist's final lonely fight. In the days
when kings and princes fell and empires shuddered, the last combat
and the deeds that transpired before it were, by their very nature, of
considerable magnitude. Their sheer size removed the tragic protagonist from ordinary people, and the disaster that followed them was total. In contrast, the actions of Blanche DuBois cause hardly a ripple beyond her circle, but her situation in no way limits the heroic size of
the deeds themselves. What is done to and by Blanche, from the "epic
fornications" of her forebears through her expulsion by the Hotel
Flamingo to her final encounter in the ludicrous jungles of the Ely-

sian Fields, is monstrous and overwhelming. Nothing takes place by
halves, for Blanche is not an insignificant creature. She has dimension,
and whatever she undertakes is undertaken to an extent far beyond
normality.

In the course of these events, tragic ironies everywhere compound
themselves. No matter what step she takes, hope for salvation this side
of the grave steadily evaporates. Seeking help, she encounters hostility;
seeking love, she encounters scornful rejection; seeking refuge, she is
driven to insanity. Every attempt to save herself by honest revelation
of her past only further enmeshes her, and the act that destroys her is
the logical ironic extension of the only behavior in the past by which
she was able to exist with a meaningful identity. In addition, throughout it all, we must recognize the absolute validity of Blanche's plea
that there are better ways than life in Stanley's cave, though to exchange it for her own world of fantasy is hardly more attractive. At
the same time, we are forced to admit that survival for Blanche—or
for anyone of sensitivity—in the grimness of existence as Williams here
portrays it depends heavily on paper shades over glaring lightbulbs
and the belief that Shep Huntleigh exists.

The final catastrophe, then, becomes overwhelming. The gods de-
mand that the protagonist be sacrificed to prove his quality, and the
realization of the greatness of the loss comes only at the moment of
liquidation. In tragedy, the death of the protagonist, symbolic or
literal, can never be a "just" death, nor can it be regarded as simply
a punishment for past misdeeds. It must be a strong, positive, and
even appropriate event, but it must also remain a passion suffered by
one doomed, one whose behavior in meeting and defying it elevates
him as it must, in the end, elevate those who watch. To observe
Blanche DuBois led away at the final curtain is not to engage in
tearful sentiment, for we are not merely beholding a pitiful, beaten
creature. Though defeated, she remains like all true tragic figures, un-
conquered, and what is asked of us is that we recognize the tragic waste,
the great pity surrounding the destruction of one whose rich humanity
can only be recognized in death. Immediately thereupon, the forces
expended in bringing her to her knees are dissipated and the balance
of things—tranquility—is restored. But this has nothing to do with a
return to the status quo, or normality, despite Stanley's insistence
that all will be as before; no tragedy permits the struggle to be forgotten. Simply, the forces of antagonism are eliminated, and the
combatants on either side now lie exhausted.

Considering the role of nemesis that he plays, Stanley is an antagonist of surprising sympathy. As so often in Williams' plays, the opposing
sides offer little choice. On the one hand is Blanche, lush, erotic,
decadent, overripe; on the other is Stanley, lusty, animalistic, earthy.

Neither attracts us, yet each arouses our compassion. If Stanley behaves like a brute, it must be acknowledged that he is, after all, defending his home, however much it may be a hovel for rutting beasts. Stanley and Stella are happy in their cave, and no amount of shocked assertion by Blanche of its lack of human sensitivities will make any difference whatever. Stanley's drinking, gambling, and instant rages are those of a petulant adolescent, but they are understandable. He is human, and he reacts very much as we might expect. Who among us would not seek every method to rid his home of an intruder bent on annihilation of his way of life? Who would not warn his best friend to avoid the clutches of a conniving bitch?

Stanley's ultimate weapon, the rape, is violently repulsive. And yet how natural for the sex-oriented Stanley to use it, the one way, as he sees it, by which his adversary can be lowered from her infuriating heights. He is not naturally a rapist, nor, for that matter, from what Williams tells us of him, is he faithless; he has his willing mate, continually in heat. He is a responsible worker and apparently a steady provider, who prefers to spend his money and spare time on poker, bowling, and beer jousts with friends, while his constant sexual needs are fulfilled by the ever-available Stella. Still, the final rape is appropriate, a totally degrading act that, ironically enough, lowers him to his victim's own level, destroying his moral superiority over her.

While the gods send their victim to slaughter by the furies, what of the others? One can see the tragic outline behind Stella and Mitch, each marked for doom, though their passive roles keep them well separated from the central antagonists.

Stella can have little before her, given this choice of life, except a steadily deteriorating existence wholly reliant upon instant passion; but her decision to remain Stanley's paramour is entirely her own. Aware that the world has progressed since men came down from trees, she still throws herself in defiant exuberant joy into Stanley's embrace to blunt Blanche's assault. She has enough pride to flee the infantile rages of her husband, but can then only return to endure more of the same. Always the pragmatist, she is content in her indolence to be the object of Stanley's studlike strutting—to endure, accept, ignore. To admit the truth would destroy her as surely as it does Blanche. Hence, our pity for her is mixed with far less compassion than we extend to her sister. When she no longer attracts, when her physical lure dies, so will she. This is not, however, our immediate concern, and so Stella remains a secondary figure.

As for Mitch, the tragic implications in his case turn out to be largely pathetic. Mother-fixated, self-conscious, desperate for manly release, he can only stumble along with a sense of propriety and decorum that is impervious to his own needs and those of Blanche. His pitiful drunken insults are the cries of a trapped animal snarling at the hand that could save him and in turn be saved by him. Honest, upright, and proper, altogether out of place in Stanley's gang of slobs, Mitch ironically turns their gross mouthings upon the creature whose own moment of honesty with him seals the doom which Stanley subsequently executes. Then back to home and mother, to a spiritual death of his own.

Perhaps the temper of these times, as Professor Krutch once said, does not support the ideas or ideals of the classic concept of tragedy. It is true, certainly, that its structure must be somewhat changed, its attitudes somewhat altered to accommodate the banality of much of contemporary experience. Possibly the strain is too great, the adaptation of moods impossible, yet to experience a good performance of *A Streetcar Named Desire* seems almost to live again the truly classical tragic outlook in what is now a "classic" American play.

IV. The Critical Spectrum

Ever since Aristotle in the fourth century B.C. observed what he felt were the essentials of tragedy and established, whether he meant to or not, the bases for dramatic evaluation millennia in the future, the theater critic has been a respected scholar, a discredited whipping boy, an inspired thinker, or a loutish dolt, depending on which side of his opinion a playwright might find himself. The critic has found respect and admiration as a guiding literary light, or has been made the butt of everything from Sheridan's witty farce of the same name to the crudest obscenities. Like eternally feuding, eternally loving couples, the theater and the critic find they cannot possibly live together, yet they know full well it is impossible to endure existence apart. The love-hate relationship between the artist and his critic is an eternal one in the arts, but in the theatre, witnessing such direct encounters as involve writer, producer, actor, technician *and* critic, the nature of the affair seems more explosively emotional, more directly personal, and more exciting to witness than anywhere else.

Tennessee Williams has always been acutely aware of the wounds which critics could impose not only upon one's pride but upon one's professional reputation, even though he well knows that the ultimate power of the reviewer in the daily press who casts his hastily composed judgments upon the early morning waters of first edition press runs cannot, actually, make or break a new play. Unlike Shaw, himself a critic of first magnitude, who could put down an adversary with wit and erudition, knowing full well that he himself was unassailable in his own knowledge of what was right or wrong; or unlike O'Neill, who would grumble privately to friends, but who refused to join the battle, preferring to bulldoze his own path in his own way, critics notwithstanding, Williams throughout his career has responded quickly, at times resentfully, against those who failed to appreciate his efforts.

In the case of *A Streetcar Named Desire,* however, Williams received what very probably may be as enthusiastic and positive an endorsement as any contemporary dramatist has received for a single new play. There were detractors, of course, but they are difficult to find in significant numbers. Wolcott Gibbs and Mary McCarthy, for instance, were notably lacking in enthusiasm, as they found Williams to lack thought, to be pseudo-poetic and inartistic, and to compose plays smelling of "careerism" (see appended bibliography). By a very wide margin, the detractors were outnumbered, and Williams has been able to bask in the sunlight of continuing critical praise of this unique creation which has not yet ceased to attract the casual reviewer, professional critic, university scholar, and medical practitioner who find in plot, theme, and character subjects for the most complex evaluation and analysis.

The first person to "criticize" *A Streetcar Named Desire* was its director, Elia Kazan. The director as we know him today is a relative newcomer to the commercial theater. Until the turn of the present century the entire career of a play more often than not was in the hands of a man who managed the company, financed the production, designed the scene, and frequently acted the leading role. In addition, he might even have owned the theatre and written the script.

Well within the last seventy-five to one hundred years, however, major changes in theatrical techniques have fostered the need for a specialist whose sole duty is to guide the play from casting through rehearsals to opening night. With the disappearance of self-contained repertory acting companies came the need to choose individual actors for each play role by role; copyright laws helped produce a body of independent dramatists who could support themselves entirely by production and publication royalties; and theater mechanics, particularly the use of electricity, hastened the elaboration of stage effects of all sorts. The physical production of a play became as important as the script, and before long the man responsible for it was a skilled and highly paid artist. Today it is not unusual for a particularly brilliant director to receive equal billing with the writer or the star.

At the beginning of his career Tennessee Williams was fortunate to have the services of two of the best directors in the business. Eddie Dowling, who also created the role of Tom, was widely credited with the success of *The Glass Menagerie.* The work of Elia Kazan was

uniformly regarded as a major contribution to *Streetcar*'s effect, and
he became inseparably associated with Williams' critical reception
until 1960, when the long association ended.

The important role of the director in a play as stylistically and
thematically complex as *Streetcar* cannot be overestimated, and Kazan's
awareness of his task is well demonstrated by the notes he wrote for
himself as the play got under way. Because the excerpts printed here
were written as personal notes not intended for publication, they provide a particularly fascinating behind-the-scenes insight into the way
the mind of a great director works.

Kazan's notes, while displaying this insight, were designed to guide
the director and were not, in the usual sense, the opinion of a "critic."
The first to react in public print, as has become customary within
this century, were the opening night reviewers. The importance of
the New York drama critics, whose brief opinions in the major daily
papers are awaited with great fear and great hope following a Broadway opening, has been debated endlessly and to no conclusion. Perhaps their weight was truly influential when a dozen or so papers
carried their comments, but now that New York has been reduced to
three major dailies (there were nine when *Streetcar* opened) the impact of the professional reviewer's pen cannot be quite the same. But,
damned or praised, the critic is an ever-present fact of life for the
New York playwright.

The three reviews of *Streetcar* reprinted in this volume are typical
of the genre. The first covers the Boston tryout and others reflect
opening-night reactions in New York. The Boston review is of particular interest considering the catastrophe which Williams experi-
enced in that city in 1940 with *Battle of Angels*. The opinions of John
Chapman and Richard Watts, Jr., whose complete reviews are in-
cluded, were widely supported by the comments of other metropolitan
New York critics, indicating how well Williams had lived down the
disaster that, seven years before, had so very nearly ended his career.

Brooks Atkinson of the *Times* regarded the play as "superb drama"
that "reveals Mr. Williams as a genuinely poetic playwright whose
knowledge of people is honest and thorough and whose sympathy is
profoundly human." Howard Barnes of the *Herald-Tribune* saw the
play as a "work of rare discernment and craftsmanship" which "becomes one of the finest plays in many seasons." William Hawkins of
the *World-Telegram* greeted it as a "terrific advance in theatre," and
Robert Coleman of the *Mirror,* while more reserved, recognized a
"dreamy, poetic, moodful vehicle . . . here on a long term lease."
George Freedley, curator of the New York Public Library Theatre
Collection, writing for the *Morning Telegraph,* found it a "drama
of great and compelling honesty," one that "has the ring of truth

and the sense of greatness," and highly recommended it to "any think-ing member of the audience." Ward Morehouse of the *Sun* regarded its "gaudy, violent, and fascinating study of the disintegration of a Southern belle" as a "full evening's worth," an "intense play packed with genuine theater." Louis Kronenberger in *PM* saw it as "the most creative new play of the season."

Whatever the playwright may think of them, the critics are always courted, and, of course, when the morning-after comments are favor-able, all's very much right with the world. To the discerning theatre-goer, however, the more cautious and detailed afterthoughts are often of greater importance in ultimate critical evaluations. Writing for later editions, particularly the Sunday entertainment supplements, the professional newspaper critic has more opportunity to ponder what he has recently seen. Seldom in this longer essay is a change of heart perceptible, but second thoughts enable the reviewer to elaborate more fully upon the opinions he was previously forced to make in haste. Once in a while he may hedge a bit, modifying a view here and there, but he will virtually never reverse an initial impression.

Our choice of three essays written for weekend editions following the opening of *Streetcar* represents opinions of three of the most im-portant and influential critics of their day. Brooks Atkinson further expands his favorable views of Williams' poetic qualities and Howard Barnes ranks the playwright with the best, on a par with Eugene O'Neill. George Jean Nathan, though not completely negative, and one who never let his close personal regard for any writer interfere with his witty, razor sharp criticism, is not entirely pleased with what he has seen.

The daily newspaper critic, both in opening night review and in Sunday supplement, provides important initial criticism of a new production, but it is pretty much an instant response required by the very nature of the publication in which it appears. The magazine columnist, however, such as Joseph Wood Krutch in the prestigious *Nation*, John Mason Brown writing regularly for *The Saturday Review*, or Irwin Shaw in the respectably leftish *New Republic*, have far better opportunities to view and criticize the play in more leisurely fashion. Prepared under less urgent deadlines, these comments be-come true essays, appearing many days or even weeks after the play has opened. In the case of *A Streetcar Named Desire*, enthusiastically welcomed by the critics of the daily press and well on its way to be-coming an important part of American stage literature, such items as those reproduced here became the first lengthy, serious critical studies in what was to develop into a long line of scholarly evaluations and judgments.

So far we have considered only the domestic review, but one cannot ignore at least a portion of the reception given *Streetcar* overseas. Even in the nineteenth century there were American playwrights who enjoyed a certain reputation outside this country. One might find a play by Bronson Howard, the first dramatist in America to earn his living solely by writing plays, on a London stage in the last decades of the century, and by the early 1900s the prolific Clyde Fitch was produced in England and on the continent. It was not until Eugene O'Neill became a genuine world figure, however, that American plays gained international stature. Between wars and immediately after, American plays had achieved a dominating influence in world drama, and *A Streetcar Named Desire* made the name of Tennessee Williams as well known to the average overseas playgoer as any contemporary playwright in any language. For all that, the play is intensely "American," and the initial reaction to it was not always parallel to the reception in New York.

In England the play was received somewhat coolly, and the review in the *Sunday Times,* reproduced here, reflects the attitude of many other London critics. P. L. Mannock of the *Daily Herald* noted somewhat favorably that "it is a wonderful story . . . the emotional effect is almost unbearably moving," and George W. Bishop in the *Daily Telegraph and Morning Post* observed that Williams is "still a poet in the use of words, his sensitive approach to character and in his use of symbolism." *The Times,* however, found the play garrulous, "perilously near to soliloquy with rare interludes of action" and observed that "Miss Vivien Leigh drifts to ruin on a tide of words many thousands strong," though the anonymous critic had to admit to the strong theatrical quality which made the play outstanding.

The appearance of Vivien Leigh, one of the finest of modern English actresses, was an excellent example of the contribution that a superior performance can bring to a production of otherwise limited appeal. Miss Leigh must surely be unique in a long list of great British actresses, for she was chosen to interpret on the screen two of America's most widely known literary heroines, both, interestingly enough, from the deep South. Her Scarlett O'Hara opposite Clark Gable in *Gone With the Wind* remains one of the classics of motion picture acting. Her role as Blanche in the remarkably faithful film adaptation of *Streetcar,* in which all other major leads were taken by those who had created the roles in the New York production, suffered very little in comparison with Jessica Tandy's original interpretation. Both performances won Miss Leigh Academy Awards.

Finally the highly entertaining review of the Paris production of *Streetcar* reveals that to say "something is lost in the translation" is more than just a truism or a worn cliché.

Even with international acclaim and a uniformly favorable domestic reception, a successful Broadway play may bring its author a fortune and may establish a new star or glorify an old one, but once its long run ends, it may also pass quickly into the pages of nostalgia and the record books. Only a few retain significance past the glamour of initial praise from newspaper critic or magazine essayist to endure as an important part of our literature. When extended essays, such as those that complete this volume, begin to appear in quarterlies and journals of restricted appeal and limited audience, as well as in books of extended literary criticism, it is safe to say that the writer and his play have "arrived" in a manner considerably beyond the showshop limits of a popular success. It did not take long for Williams, particularly through *A Streetcar Named Desire,* to gain recognition as a significant contributor to American dramatic literature.

Williams' female characters have, quite naturally, been the subject of considerable critical interest. One of the best studies of the entire gallery is from an essay by the late Durant da Ponte which appeared in *Tennessee Studies in Literature.* It is unfortunate that space limitations force our restriction here to the portions concerning only Blanche, for each woman whom Williams has created is a fascinating object indeed. An examination of Blanche as a prostitute is contained in Dr. Philip Weissman's article, which provides an interesting viewpoint through the eyes of a psychologist rather than a literary critic. The influence of the great German philosopher Nietzsche as observed by Joseph N. Riddell completes our trio of examples from this genre of criticism.

The final three, rather substantial essays are taken from books of a broader nature than the single essay in a publication. In 1955 W. David Sievers wrote a detailed study of the influence of Freudian thought in contemporary American drama in a volume called *Freud on Broadway.* Professor Sievers considered even at this fairly early date that Williams and *Streetcar* were important enough for lengthy comment. Then, by 1962 Williams had earned a place in Twayne Publishers' United States Authors Series, which Signi Falk was chosen to write. Finally, a younger generation of scholars from overseas, represented by Christopher W. E. Bigsby, writing in 1969 for a collection of essays on literature of the 1940s, had begun to regard Williams as one of the most outstanding figures in modern drama, worthy of permanent residence on Parnassus as a major contributor to world dramatic literature.

PART ONE

The Play as Commercial Theater

Elia Kazan: Notebook for A Streetcar Named Desire

A thought—directing finally consists of turning Psychology into Behavior.

Theme—this is a message from the dark interior. This little twisted, pathetic, confused bit of light and culture puts out a cry. It is snuffed out by the crude forces of violence, insensibility and vulgarity which exist in our South—and this cry is the play.

Style—one reason a "style," a stylized production is necessary is that a subjective factor—Blanche's memories, inner life, emotions, are a real factor. We cannot really understand her behavior unless we see the effect of her past on her present behavior.

This play is a poetic tragedy. We are shown the final dissolution of a person of worth, who once had great potential, and who, even as she goes down, has worth exceeding that of the "healthy," coarse-grained figures who kill her. . . .

The style—the real deep style—consists of one thing only: to find behavior that's truly social, significantly typical, at each moment. It's not so much what Blanche has done—it's how she does it—with such style, grace, manners, old-world trappings and effects, props, tricks, swirls, etc., that they seem anything but vulgar.

And for the other characters, too, you face the same problem. To find the Don Quixote character for them. *This is a poetic tragedy, not a realistic or a naturalistic one. So you must find a Don Quixote scheme of things for each.* . . .

Excerpts taken from Elia Kazan's "Notebook for A Streetcar Named Desire*" published in* Directors on Directing, *edited by Toby Cole and Helen Krich Chinoy, The Bobbs-Merrill Company, Inc., Indianapolis, 1963. Reprinted by permission of The Bobbs-Merrill Company, Inc., and the editors.*

Blanche

"Blanche is Desperate"

"This is the End of the Line of the Streetcar Named Desire"

Spine—find Protection: the tradition of the old South says that it must be through another person.

Her problem has to do with her tradition. Her notion of what a woman should be. She is stuck with this "ideal." It is her. It is her ego. Unless she lives by it, she cannot live; in fact her whole life has been for nothing. . . .
Because this image of herself cannot be accomplished in reality, certainly not in the South of our day and time, it is her effort and practice to *accomplish it in fantasy.* Everything that she does in *reality* too is colored by this necessity, this compulsion to be *special.* So, in fact, *reality becomes fantasy too.* She makes it so!

The variety essential to the play . . . demands that she be a "heavy" at the beginning. For instance: contemplate the inner character contradiction: bossy yet helpless, domineering yet shaky, etc. The audience at the beginning should see her bad effect on Stella, want Stanley to tell her off. He does. He exposes her and then gradually, as they see how genuinely in pain, how actually desperate she is, how warm, tender and loving she can be (the Mitch story), how freighted with need she is—then they begin to go with her. They begin to realize that they are sitting in at the death of something extraordinary . . . colorful, varied, passionate, lost, witty, imaginative, of her own integrity . . . and then they feel the tragedy. In the playing too there can be a growing sincerity and directness.

The thing about the "tradition" in the nineteenth century was that *it worked then.* It made a woman feel important with her own secure positions and functions, her own special worth. It also made a woman at that time *one with her society.* But *today* the tradition is an anachronism which simply does not function. *It does not work.* So while Blanche must believe it because it makes her special, because it makes her sticking by Belle Reve an act of heroism, rather than an absurd romanticism, still *it does not work.* . . . She's a misfit, a liar, her "airs" alienate people, she must act superior to them which alienates them further. She doesn't know how to work. So she can't make a living.

She's really helpless. She needs someone to help her. Protection. She's a last dying relic of the last century now adrift in our unfriendly day. . . .

If this is a romantic tragedy, what is its inevitability and what is the tragic flaw? In the Aristotelian sense, the flaw is the need to be superior, special (or *her* need for protection and what it means to her), the "tradition." This creates an apartness so intense, a loneliness so gnawing that only a complete breakdown, a refusal, as it were, to contemplate what she's doing, a *binge* as it were, a destruction of all her standards, a desperate violent ride on the Streetcar Named Desire can break through the walls of her tradition. The tragic flaw creates the circumstances, inevitably, that destroy her. . . .

There is another, simpler and equally terrible contradiction in her own nature. She won't face her physical or sensual side. She calls it "brutal desire." She thinks she sins when she gives in to it . . . yet she does give in to it, out of loneliness . . . but by calling it "brutal desire," she is able to separate it from her "real self," her "cultured," refined self. Her tradition makes no allowance, allows no space for this very real part of herself. So she is constantly in conflict, not at ease, sinning. *She's still looking for something that doesn't exist today, a gentleman,* who will treat her like a virgin, marry her, protect her, defend and maintain her honor, etc. She wants an old-fashioned wedding dressed in white . . . and still she does things out of "brutal desire" that make this impossible. *All this too is tradition.*

She has worth too—she is better than Stella. She says: ". . . In this dark march toward whatever it is we're approaching . . . don't . . . don't hang back with the brutes!" And though the direct psychological motivation for this is jealousy and personal frustration, still she, alone and abandoned in the crude society of New Orleans back streets, is the *only voice of light.* It is flickering and, in the course of the play, goes out. But it is valuable because it is unique.

Blanche is a butterfly in a jungle looking for just a little momentary protection, doomed to a sudden, early violent death. The more I work on Blanche, incidentally, the less insane she seems. She is caught in a fatal inner contradiction, but in another society, she *would* work. In Stanley's society, no!

This is like a classic tragedy. Blanche is Medea or someone pursued by the Harpies, the Harpies being *her own nature.* Her inner sickness pursues her like *doom* and makes it impossible for her to attain the one thing she needs, the only thing she needs: a safe harbor. . . .

Blanche is an outdated creature, approaching extinction . . . like the dinosaur. She is about to be pushed off the edge of the earth. On the other hand she is a heightened version, an artistic intensification of all women. That is what makes the play universal. Blanche's special relation to all women is that she is at that critical point where *the one thing above all else that she is dependent on: her attraction for men, is beginning to go.* Blanche is like all women, dependent on a man, looking for one to hang onto: only *more so!*

. . . Is it any wonder that she tries to attract each and every man she meets. She'll even take that protected feeling, that needed feeling, that superior feeling, for a moment. Because, at least for a moment, that anxiety, the hurt and the pain will be quenched. The sex act is the opposite of loneliness. Desire is the opposite of Death. . . .

Compelled by her nature (she must be special, superior) she makes it impossible with Stanley and Stella. She acts in a way that succeeds in being destructive. But the last bit of luck is with her. She finds the only man on earth whom she suits, a man who is looking for a dominant woman. For an instant she is happy. But her past catches up with her. Stanley, whom she's antagonized by her destructiveness aimed at his home, but especially by her need to be superior, uses her past, which he digs up, to destroy her. Finally she takes refuge in fantasy. She must have protection, closeness, love, safe harbor. The only place she can obtain them any longer is in her own mind. She "goes crazy."

Stella

Spine—hold onto Stanley (Blanche the antagonist).

One reason Stella submits to Stanley's solution at the end, is perfectly ready to, is that she has an unconscious hostility toward Blanche. Blanche is so patronizing, demanding and superior toward her . . . makes her so useless, old-fashioned and helpless . . . everything that Stanley has got her out of. Stanley has made a woman out of her. Blanche immediately returns her to the subjugation of childhood, younger-sister-ness.

Stella would have been Blanche except for Stanley. She now knows what, how much Stanley means to her health. So . . . no matter what

Stanley does . . . she must cling to him, as she does to life itself. To
return to Blanche would be to return to the subjugation of the tradition. . . .

Stella is a refined girl who has found a kind of salvation or realization, *but at a terrific price.* She keeps her eyes closed, even stays in
bed as much as possible so that she won't realize, won't *feel* the pain
of this terrific price. She walks around as if narcotized, as if sleepy, as
if in a daze. She is waiting for night. She's waiting for the dark where
Stanley makes her feel *only him* and she has no reminder of the price
she is paying. She wants no intrusion from the other world. . . .

She has a paradise—a serenely limited paradise when Blanche enters—but Blanche makes her consider Stanley, judge Stanley and find
him wanting, for the first time. But it is too late. In the end she returns to Stanley.

Stella is doomed too. She has sold herself out for a temporary solution. She's given up all hope, everything, just to live for Stanley's
pleasures. So she is dependent on Stanley's least whim. But this can
last only as long as Stanley wants her. And *secondly* and *chiefly*—
Stella herself cannot live narcotized forever. There is more to her.
She begins to feel, even in the sex act, *taken,* unfulfilled—not recognized . . . and besides she's deeper, needs more variety. Her only hope
is her children and, like so many women, she will begin to live more
and more for her children.

Stella, at the beginning of the play, won't face a *hostility* (concealed
from herself and unrecognized) toward Stanley. . . . Latent in Stella
is rebellion. Blanche arouses it.

Stella is plain out of her head about Stanley. . . . He is her first
man, really; he made her a woman. He fulfilled her more than she
knew possible and she has to stop herself from *crawling* after him.
She's utterly *blind* as to what's wrong with Stanley. She's blind to it
and she doesn't care, *until* Blanche arrives. At the end of the play,
her life is entirely different. It will never be the same with Stanley
again.

Note from Tennessee Williams on the fourth day of rehearsal:
"Gadge—I am a bit concerned over Stella in Scene One. It seems to
me that she has too much vivacity, at times she is bouncing around in
a way that suggests a co-ed on a benzedrine kick. I know it is impossible to be literal about the description 'narcotized tranquillity' but I

do think there is an important value in suggesting it, in contrast to Blanche's rather feverish excitability. . . ."

Stanley

Spine—keep things his way (Blanche the antagonist).

The hedonist, objects, props, etc. Sucks on a cigar all day because he can't suck a teat. Fruit, food, etc. He's got it all figured out, what fits, what doesn't. The pleasure scheme. He has all the confidence of resurgent flesh.

Also with a kind of naïveté . . . even slowness . . . he means no harm. He wants to knock no one down. He only doesn't want to be taken advantage of. His code is simple and simple-minded. He is adjusted *now* . . . later, as his sexual powers die, so will he; the trouble will come later, the "problems."

But what is the chink in his armor now, the contradiction? Why does Blanche get so completely under his skin? Why does he want to bring Blanche and, before her, Stella *down to his level?* . . . It's the hoodlum aristocrat. He's deeply dissatisfied, deeply hopeless, deeply cynical . . . the physical immediate pleasures, if they come in a steady enough stream quiet this *as long as no one gets more* . . . then his bitterness comes forth and he tears down the pretender. But Blanche he can't seem to do anything with. She can't come down to his level so he levels her with his sex. He brings her right down to his level, beneath him.

One of the important things for Stanley is that Blanche *would wreck his home*. Blanche is dangerous. She is destructive. . . .

The one thing that Stanley can't bear is someone who thinks that he or she is better than he. His only way of explaining himself—he thinks he stinks—is that everyone else stinks. This is symbolic. True of our National State of Cynicism. No values. There is nothing to command his loyalty. Stanley rapes Blanche because he has tried and tried to keep her down to his level. This way is the last. . . .

. . . Emphasize Stanley's love for Stella. It is rough, embarrassed and he rather truculently *won't show it*. But it is there. He's proud of her. When he's not on guard and looking at her his eyes suddenly shine. He is grateful too, proud, satisfied. But he'd never show it, demonstrate it.

Stanley is supremely indifferent to everything except his own pleasure and comfort. He is marvelously selfish, a miracle of sensuous self-centeredness. He builds a hedonist life, and fights to the death to defend it—but finally it is *not* enough to hold Stella

and

this philosophy is not successful even for him—because every once in a while the silenced, frustrated part of Stanley breaks loose in unexpected and unpredictable ways and we suddenly see, as in a burst of lightning, his real frustrated self. Usually his frustration is worked off by eating a lot, drinking a lot, gambling a lot, fornicating a lot. He's going to get very fat later. He's desperately trying to squeeze out happiness by living by *ball and jowl* . . . and it really doesn't work . . . because it simply stores up violence and stores up violence, until *every bar in the nation is full of Stanleys ready to explode*. He's desperately trying to drug his senses . . . overwhelming them with a constant round of sensation so that he will feel nothing else.

In Stanley sex goes under a disguise. Nothing is more erotic and arousing to him than "airs" . . . she thinks she's better than me . . . I'll show her. . . . Sex equals domination . . . anything that challenges him—like calling him "common"—arouses him sexually. . . .

As a character Stanley is most interesting in his "contradictions," his "soft" moments, his sudden pathetic little-tough-boy tenderness toward Stella. Scene 3 he cries like a baby. Somewhere in Scene 8 he almost makes it up with Blanche. In Scene 10 he *does* try to make it up with her—and except for her doing the one thing that most arouses him, both in anger and sex, he might have.

Elinor Hughes: Review of tryout performance
in Boston

Tennessee Williams, winner of all manner of prizes for his play of two years ago, "The Glass Menagerie," is with us again, presenting the most haunting new drama, "A Streetcar Named Desire." To compare him with any current playwright is impossible, for he has a quality completely and uniquely his own—the ability to tell a pitiful,

Review of tryout performance in Boston by Elinor Hughes. From The Boston
Herald, *November 4, 1947. Reprinted by permission of* The Boston Herald.

always believable and nakedly honest story in terms of moods, snatches
of speech, emotions suggested. Plot in the usual sense there is not
too much of, for it is men and women in their moods of hope, despair,
pretence, terror and uncertainty with whom he is concerned. Yet the
play is purposeful and it held Monday night's audience tense and si-
lent to the final curtain. Elia Kazan's direction seemed to me evocative
and brilliant, and Irene M. Selznick, the producer, is to be congrat-
ulated upon bringing to the theater so striking and unusual a script.

Taking his title from the streetcar that runs through the Vieux
Carre in New Orleans, a streetcar that bears the name of Desire and
connects with another streetcar named Cemetery, the playwright tells
the story of Blanche Du Bois, frail, pretty, rather too fine drawn and
over-elegant, who arrives suddenly on the doorstep of her young sister,
Stella, and Stella's forthright unimpressionable husband, Stanley Kowalski. Her arrival brings nothing but clashes and confusion; her talk
—about her nerves, her teaching and the old plantations, now lost,
where she and Stella had grown up—has a baffling quality about it,
as though there were ultimate truths that she could not speak. Soon
she has put Stella and Stanley outwardly at odds with one another.
She talks of her conquests, she is afraid of bright lights and responds
rather desperately to the clumsy, polite advances of Stanley's friend,
Mitch, who thinks he would like to marry her.

The hot summer days idle by, but the tension grows: Stella's baby
is coming and Stanley, frantic to be rid of Blanche, finally unearths
the truth about her that, once published abroad, is to destroy her. A
tragic early marriage, ending in disaster, had driven her to more
and more men, to drink, and to taking refuge in a dream world where
what mattered was not truth but what she wanted to be true.

There seem no words adequate to describe the remarkable performance by Jessica Tandy as the tragic Blanche, for this is really
superb, imaginative and illuminating acting. With rare skill she suggests a lost, pitiful and confused woman, clinging to the illusion of
beauty, clutching at the shadows of happiness, seeking to fly from
the terrors of her lost love and family disaster.

The play is largely hers, but the other performances are most excellent; Marlon Brando fulfills his earlier promise with a mature and
forceful performance of the angry, boisterous, resentful Stanley, seeking to salvage through brutality his resentment of Blanche's conde-
scension. Kim Hunter is appealing and lovable as young Stella, torn
between love for her husband and pity for her sister. Karl Malden
brings strength and honesty to the role of Mitch.

The lesser roles, those of the quarrelsome but kind-hearted Hubbels,
are well taken by Peg Hillias and Rudy Bond; Donald Oenslager's

transparent walled setting is imaginatively conceived and lighted and the background music is haunting and effective throughout.

John Chapman: *Streetcar Named Desire* Sets Season's High in Acting, Writing

Tennessee Williams, a young playwright who is not ashamed of being a poet, has given us a superb drama in "A Streetcar Named Desire." Last evening, under the sentient direction of Elia Kazan, it was given a brilliant performance at the Ethel Barrymore Theatre. The company, headed by Jessica Tandy, Marlon Brando, Kim Hunter and Karl Malden, is the answer to a playgoer's prayer.

Williams came upon the theatrical scene with "The Glass Menagerie," a delicate, haunting and tender dramatic fragment which marked him as a writer to be reckoned with. This promise of more to come, and better to come, has been fulfilled in his new work. "Menagerie" was memorably performed by the late Laurette Taylor, Eddie Dowling, Julie Haydon and Anthony Ross; "A Streetcar Named Desire" comes warmly to life in the playing—and it is certain now that Williams writes actable dramas.

"The Glass Menagerie" was, as I have said, a fragment, a cameo. The new play is full-scale—throbbingly alive, compassionate, heart-wrenchingly human. It has the tragic overtones of grand opera, and is, indeed, the story of a New Orleans Camille—a wistful little trollop who shuns the reality of what she is and takes gallant and desperate refuge in a magical life she has invented for herself.

In New Orleans there are, Mr. Williams has pointed out, two streetcars, one named Desire, the other Cemetery, and this is a theme of his play. To Blanche du Bois, a schoolteacher in her thirties, death is one thing and the other end of the line is not just life, but desire.

When one meets her she has taken the car named Desire to visit the sleazy but happy "quarter" home of her sister, who is married to a stalwart Polish–American whose enthusiasms run to bowling, beer, poker and whisky. He is a realist, is Stanley Kowalski—and Blanche is in flight from reality.

She has come, she tells her sister, because she has not been well. She has taken leave of absence from her teaching job back in their

"Streetcar Named Desire *Sets Season's High in Acting, Writing"* by John Chapman. *Review of opening night performance in New York, from* The New York Daily News, *December 4, 1947. Reprinted by permission of* The Daily News.

home in Mississippi. Once the girls had a fine house there, but it has
slipped from Blanche's hands—just how is never made clear, for
Blanche is not one for facts.

This dream world of hers is beautiful—but terrifying, as one comes
to see the person Blanche really is. She is the Hatrack of her Mississippi
town; a generous, loving accommodator of any yearning stranger who
has been driven out. But in her own mind she is a lady of purest ray
serene and her trunk of shoddy carnival raiment and rhinestone tiaras
is the finest of the fine. She is a pitiful figure and her story is told
with pity and acted gloriously by Miss Tandy; and there is heartbreak
in the theatre when, broken but ever so gallant, she is led away to a
place where dreamers may dream out their lives.

Mr. Williams has set his tale against a colorful, noisy, lustily humorous background—the generous and earthy life of a New Orleans
tenement. From across the street there comes into the Kowalskis' two
small rooms the music of a honky-tonk. Into the rooms, too, come
the Kowalskis' friends, including a gentle man who finds in Blanche
the girl of girls—until he sees her in the bright light of actuality.

Mr. Brando is magnificent as the forthright husband, in his simple
rages, his simple affections and his blunt humor. Admirable is Miss
Hunter as Blanche's easygoing sister, and Mr. Malden is splendid as
the shy admirer. Mr. Williams has skillfully combined the touch of
a poet with the practicality of a dramatic craftsman, and Jo Mielziner
has housed "A Streetcar Named Desire" in an extraordinarily effective setting. The production marks the managerial debut here of
Irene Selznick, who had the grace and wisdom to turn it over to Mr.
Kazan to bring it into being.

Richard Watts, Jr.: Streetcar Named Desire Is Striking Drama

Tennessee Williams' new play is a feverish, squalid, tumultuous,
painful, steadily arresting and oddly touching study of feminine decay
along the lower Mississippi. Brilliantly staged by Elia Kazan and ably
acted by Jessica Tandy and some other good players, "A Streetcar
Named Desire" last night added notably to the color and excitement
of the theatrical season, demonstrated once more the skill of its director and actors, and indicated again that Mr. Williams is an on-

"Streetcar Named Desire *Is Striking Drama" by Richard Watts, Jr. From* The
New York Post, *December 4, 1947. Reprinted by permission of the* New York Post.
Copyright © 1947, 1950, New York Post Corporation.

coming playwright of power, imagination and almost desperately morbid turn of mind and emotion. In his latest work to reach Broadway,
the dramatist is telling the story of a doomed Southern girl who seems
startlingly like what the foolish old mother of his previous drama,
"The Glass Menagerie," might well have been at a similar age. Hers,
to put it mildly, is not a pleasant life story. Essentially a romantic
and dreamy young woman, it is her fate to represent in her frail spirit
the decline and fall of a long line of decadent Southern aristocrats,
and, for all her sentimental imagination, she ends as a simpering, wit-
less prostitute.

Two characteristic traits of Mr. Williams' morbid imagination are
distinguishable in his new play. I should say that one was admirable
and the other less praiseworthy. Despite the blackness of fate which
he depicts, there is a frequent quality of lyric originality in his pessimism that gives it an inescapable vitality. Things may look depressing
to him, but there is always the rich tumult of life to make up for it.
On the other hand, his doomed heroines are so helplessly enmeshed
in their fate they cannot put up a properly dramatic battle against it.

There is something a little embarrassing about watching the torment
of as helpless a victim of a playwright's brooding imagination as the
heroine of "A Streetcar Named Desire," particularly when her downfall is studied with almost loving detail. The result is that the play
has a painful, rather pitiful quality about it. Yet its characters are so
knowingly and understandably presented, the vividness of its life is
so compelling, and the theatrical skill of its portrait of spiritual and
moral decay so impressive that it never ceases to be effective and
powerful.

In the long and difficult central role, Jessica Tandy, invariably an
interesting actress, is always deeply moving, even though she starts
with a considerable handicap. For the truth is that she doesn't manage
to suggest a chattering, coquettish girl from the deep South to any
one's satisfaction. It is all the more a tribute to her, therefore, that
the honesty and sensitivity of her playing are great enough to make
the defect in type casting unimportant.

I have hitherto not shared the enthusiasm of most reviewers for
Marlon Brando, but his portrayal of the heroine's sullen, violent nemesis is an excellent piece of work. Even finer, though, is Karl Malden,
one of the ablest young actors extant, as the girl's sentimental and
disillusioned admirer. There is likewise a good performance by Kim
Hunter as the less complex sister of the lost neurotic. Everything
about the production of "A Streetcar Named Desire" has gone well,
including the setting, lighting and costumes, and the result is one of
the events of the season.

Brooks Atkinson: "Streetcar" Tragedy—Mr. Williams' Report on Life in New Orleans

By common consent, the finest new play on the boards just now is Tennessee Williams' "A Streetcar Named Desire." As a tribute to the good taste of this community, it is also a smash hit. This combination of fine quality and commercial success is an interesting phenomenon. For if the literal facts of the story could be considered apart from Mr. Williams' imaginative style of writing, "Streetcar" might be clattering through an empty theatre. It is not a popular play, designed to attract and entertain the public. It cannot be dropped into any of the theatre's familiar categories. It has no plot, at least in the familiar usage of that word. It is almost unbearably tragic.

After attending a play of painful character, theatregoers frequently ask in self-defense: "What's the good of harrowing people like that?" No one can answer that sort of question. The usual motives for self-expression do not obtain in this instance. There is no purpose in "Streetcar." It solves no problems; it arrives at no general moral conclusions. It is the rueful character portrait of one person, Blanche Du Bois of Mississippi and New Orleans. Since she is created on the stage as a distinct individual, experiences identical with hers can never be repeated. She and the play that is woven about her are unique. For Mr. Williams is not writing of representative men and women; he is not a social author absorbed in the great issues of his time and, unlike timely plays, "Streetcar" does not acquire stature or excitement from the world outside the theatre.

These negative comments are introduced to establish some perspective by which "Streetcar" may be appreciated as a work of art. As a matter of fact, people do appreciate it thoroughly. They come away from it profoundly moved and also in some curious way elated. For they have been sitting all evening in the presence of truth, and that is a rare and wonderful experience. Out of nothing more esoteric than interest in human beings, Mr. Williams has looked steadily and wholly into the private agony of one lost person. He supplies dramatic conflict by introducing Blanche to an alien environment that brutally wears on her nerves. But he takes no sides in the conflict. He knows how right all the characters are—how right she is in trying to protect herself against the disaster that is overtaking her, and how right the other characters are in protecting their independence, for her terrible needs cannot be fulfilled. There is no solution except the painful one Mr. Williams provides in his last scene.

For Blanche is not just a withered remnant of Southern gentility. She is in flight from a world she could not control and which has done frightful things to her. She has stood by during a long siege of deaths in the family, each death having robbed her of strength and plunged her further into loneliness. Her marriage to an attractive boy who looked to her for spiritual security was doomed from the start; and even if she had been a superwoman she could not have saved it.

By the time we see her in the play she is hysterical from a long and shattering ordeal. In the wildness of her dilemma she clings desperately to illusions of refinement—pretty clothes that soothe her ego, perfumes and ostentatious jewelry, artifices of manners, forms and symbols of respectability. Since she does not believe in herself, she tries to create a false world in which she can hide. But she is living with normal people who find her out and condemn her by normal standards. There is no hope for Blanche. Even if her wildest dreams came true, even if the rich man who has become her obsession did rescue her, she would still be lost. She will always have to flee reality.

Although Mr. Williams does not write verse nor escape into mysticism or grandeur, he is a poet. There is no fancy writing in "Streetcar." He is a poet because he is aware of people and of life. His perceptions are quick. Out of a few characters he can evoke the sense of life as a wide, endlessly flowing pattern of human needs and aspirations. Although "Streetcar" is specific about its characters and episodes, it is not self-contained. The scenes of present time, set in a New Orleans tenement, have roots in the past, and you know that Mr. Williams' characters are going on for years into some mysterious future that will always be haunted by the wounding things we see on the stage. For he is merely recording a few lacerating weeks torn out of time. He is an incomparably beautiful writer, not because the words are lustrous, but because the dialogue is revealing and sets up overtones. Although he has confined truth to one small and fortuitous example, it seems to have the full dimensions of life on the stage. It almost seems not to have been written but to be happening.

"Streetcar" deserves the devotion of the theatre's most skillful craftsmen; and, not entirely by accident, it has acquired them. Elia Kazan, who brilliantly directed "All My Sons" last season, is versatile enough to direct "Streetcar" brilliantly also. He has woven the tenderness and the brutality into a single strand of spontaneous motion. Confronted with the task of relating the vivid reality of "Streetcar" to its background in the city and to its awareness of life in general, Jo Mielziner has designed a memorable, poetic setting with a deep range of tones.

The acting cannot be praised too highly. Marlon Brando's braggart, sullen, caustic brother-in-law, Karl Malden's dull-witted, commonplace suitor, Kim Hunter's affectionate, level-headed sister are vivid character portraits done with freshness and definition. As Blanche Du Bois, Jessica Tandy has one of the longest and most exacting parts on record. She plays it with an insight as vibrant and pitiless as Mr. Williams' writing, for she catches on the wing the terror, the bogus refinement, the intellectual alertness and the madness that can hardly be distinguished from logic and fastidiousness. Miss Tandy acts a magnificent part magnificently.

It is no reflection on the director and the actors to observe that Mr. Williams has put into his script everything vital we see on the stage. A workman as well as an artist, he has not only imagined the whole drama but set it down on paper where it can be read. The script is a remarkably finished job: it describes the characters at full length, it foresees the performance, the impact of the various people on each other, the contrasts in tone of their temperaments and motives.

In comparison with "The Glass Menagerie," "Streetcar" is a more coherent and lucid drama without loose ends, and the mood is more firmly established. "Summer and Smoke," which has not yet been produced in New York, has wider range and divides the main interest between two principal characters. If it is staged and acted as brilliantly as the performance of "Streetcar," it ought to supply the third item in a notable trilogy. For there is considerable uniformity in the choice of characters and in the attitude toward life. That uniformity may limit the range of Mr. Williams' career as a playwright; so far, he has succeeded best with people who are much alike in spirit. In the meantime, he has brought into the theatre the gifts of a poetic writer and a play that is conspicuously less mortal than most.

Howard Barnes: O'Neill Status Won by Author of "Streetcar"

A great new talent is at work in the theater to make one hope that the lean years are over. In "A Streetcar Named Desire" Tennessee Williams more than justifies the promise of high dramatic imagination and craftsmanship which he held forth in "The Glass Menagerie." His new work is a somber tragedy about frustration, but it has

"*O'Neill Status Won by Author of 'Streetcar'*" *by Howard Barnes. From* The New York Herald Tribune, *December 14, 1947, Sec. V, p. 1. Copyright © 1947, New York Herald Tribune, Inc. Reprinted with permission of W. C. C. Publishing Company, Inc.*

far more heroic dimensions than his earlier Broadway exhibit. There is a maturity about the offering at the Ethel Barrymore Theater which is the product of discipline, integrity, and experience. Where "The Glass Menagerie" was provocative, "A Streetcar Named Desire" is solid as well as perceptive; moving as well as engrossing.

Williams is certainly the Eugene O'Neill of the present period on the stage. His somewhat rugged background permits him to view the passing scene with acute and compassionate observation. An immense amount of writing, little of which has realized theatrical projection, has given him a defined style. He has an ear for dialogue and he has the artistry to translate the yak-yak of ordinary conversation into incisive and communicative passages. Judged merely on his previous Broadway plays, one might have expected him to fancy symbolism rather than honest reconstruction of human experience. He has avoided that pitfall magnificently in "A Streetcar Named Desire."

Whatever his inspiration for that drama may have been while he was living in a cheap boarding house in New Orleans and listening to a couple of trolleys called "Desire" and "Cemetery" clanging past his bedroom window, he has let it color his title rather than the substance of his writing. His approach to a savage and poignant case history of a woman's degradation is terse and terrifying at the Ethel Barrymore. Here is a playwright who loves and understands people and wants them to be more eloquent and appealing than they would be in the terrible reality of a squalid rooming house on the Vieux Carre. He has succeeded in giving them curiously extraordinary stature.

Perhaps the chief distinction of a dramatist who must be counted right at the top of the heap in the contemporary theater is his resolute disregard for so-called social problems. The prostitute who is the central figure in his play is a product of the decaying South. Coming from Mississippi by easy bordello stages to her sister's flat in New Orleans, she might have been employed to voice some economic or political theories in the course of her gradual degeneration. But Williams accepts the facts of a dislocated world in more than one scene, without belaboring the causes for a forlorn society. On the contrary, he paints his figure of Blanche du Bois, pretending to a vanished culture and grasping at a return to normalcy, in the bold strokes of enduring dramaturgy.

At the same time, he fills his show with such lusty vitality that it almost never has a fin-de-siècle touch. Blanche's sister, who has welcomed marriage to a tough factory worker of Polish descent and does not care if he beats the daylights out of her, is as vibrant a belle as one might wish to encounter. Her husband is strictly animal in his instincts, his actions and his views of living. There is nothing desiccated about "A Streetcar Named Desire," even to the central character of the piece. When she finally goes daft, after her brother-in-law has violated her, the scene has a cruel precision.

A play of stature has been given fully dimensioned representation at the Ethel Barrymore. Jessica Tandy plays the leading role of the bemused stray with exciting modulations. Her desperate deceits, as she tries to hold on to some stability of living in her sister's apartment and almost marries a young man with a mother fixation, are mirrored with clarity and terrible emphasis in a brilliant performance. Even the scenes which find her recounting her marriage to a pervert, as she tries to understand her personal tragedy, are sustained with extraordinary effect. Williams might have done some judicious cutting on one or two of these interludes, but Miss Tandy never fails his script.

Marlon Brando is close to matching her portrayal as the very physical brother-in-law, and Kim Hunter is completely convincing and singularly engaging as the sister who has settled for sex. Then there are Karl Malden, contributing an arresting bit as the gentleman caller, and a number of other lesser players who build in the corners of a starkly realistic drama. Elia Kazan has produced and directed the work with a sensitive understanding of both its depth and its surface luster, while Jo Mielziner has devised a setting which is nothing short of triumphant to frame the action. Williams is on the right track. He has had wonderful assistance in the production of his new play. It is not unlikely that he will lead the theater into a new and exciting era.

George Jean Nathan: The Streetcar Isn't Drawn by Pegasus

Tennessee Williams' "A Streetcar Named Desire," or "The Glands Menagerie," has been described in some quarters as an unpleasant play. The description is accurate; it is. But the fact that a play is unpleasant is, needless to say, not necessarily a reflection on its quality. "Oedipus," "Lear" and "The Lower Depths," to name only three out of many, are surely very far from pleasant, yet it is their unpleasantness which at least in part makes them what they are. There is a considerable difference between the unpleasant and the disgusting, which is the designation Williams' critics probably have in mind, and his play is not disgusting, as, for example, is such scum as "Maid In The Ozarks" and "School For Brides."

"The Streetcar Isn't Drawn by Pegasus" by George Jean Nathan. From The New York Journal-American, *December 15, 1947. Reprinted by permission of Julie Haydon Nathan.*

The borderline between the unpleasant and the disgusting is, however, a shadowy one, as inferior playwrights have at times found out to their surprise and grief. Williams has managed to keep his play wholly in hand. But there is, too, a much more shadowy borderline between the unpleasant and the enlightening, and Williams has tripped over it, badly. While he has succeeded in making realistically dramatic such elements as sexual abnormality, harlotry, perversion, seduction and lunacy, he has scarcely contrived to distil from them any elevation and purge. His play as a consequence remains largely a theatrical shocker which, while it may shock the emotions of its audience, doesn't in the slightest shock them into any spiritual education.

Seven years ago, at the start of his career, Williams wrote a play called "Battle of Angels," which closed in Boston after a brief showing. It hinted at his preoccupation with sex in its more violent aspects, which continues in the present exhibit. It also, while not so able a play, betrayed his apparent conviction that theatrical sensationalism and dramatic substantiality are much the same thing and that you can handily pass the former off for the latter, and for something pretty artistic into the bargain, by gilding it with occasional literary flourishes accompanied by off-stage vibra-harps, flutes and music boxes. The hanky-panky may work with a susceptible public, but not with the more snooping criticism. There is a considerable difference between Wedekind and Wedekindergarten.

To fashion any such festering materials into important drama it is essential that they be lifted out of life into a pattern larger than life, as, among others, Strindberg and his contemporary disciple, O'Neill, have appreciated. Williams in considerable part leaves them where he found them and deludes himself into a belief that he has made the gutter into a broad sea by sailing in it little papier-mache poesy boats, propelled by doughty exhalations.

Impressionistically, the play suggests a wayward bus occupied by John Steinbeck, William Faulkner and James Cain, all tipsy and all telling stories simultaneously, and with Williams, cocking his ear to assimilate the goings-on, as the conductor. Critically, it suggests that he is a little deaf and has not been able to disentangle what may be valid from the bedlam and to assimilate it to possibly reputable ends. Theatrically and popularly, however, the result will surely impress a lot of people, even such as will pretend for appearances' sake to be offended by what they allude to as its "strong meat" and who after seeing it will profess that they long for a breath of fresh, good, clean glue.

Like a number of his contemporaries, Williams seems to labor under the misapprehension that strong emotions are best to be expressed strongly only through what may politely be termed strong language. I am not, you may be relieved to know, going to take up again the already over-argued question as to whether such language has any literary justification. I am as tired of the discussion as undoubtedly you are. But, justified or not in certain cases, it seems to me that in this specific instance he has at times used it not because it is vitally necessary but for purposes of startle and because his dramatic gifts do not yet include the ability to achieve the desired effect without easy recourse to such spade-label terminology.

The play centers on a Southern school-teacher whose youthful marriage ended in tragedy when her maladjusted husband committed suicide, who has vainly sought release in miscellaneous sex, and who has become an incurable neurotic with delusions of grandeur. It develops her amorous life with her sister's husband and with the latter's crony. And it ends with her mental disintegration and deposit in an asylum. That it holds one's interest isn't to be denied. But it holds it much as it is perversely held by a recognizably fixed prizefight or a circus performer projected out of what appears to be a booming cannon by a mechanical spring device. It is, in other words, highly successful theatre and highly successful showmanship, but considerably less than that as critically secure drama.

Contributing greatly to the external successful aspects of the play are admirable direction by Elia Kazan and a uniformly excellent acting company in which, supported by Marlon Brando, Karl Malden and the others, Jessica Tandy as Forever Streetcar gives one of the finest performances observed here in some seasons.

Joseph Wood Krutch: Review of *Streetcar Named Desire*

Two years ago when Tennessee Williams was being hailed as the best new playwright to appear in a decade I was among those who were inclined to wait and see, but "A Streetcar Named Desire" (Barrymore Theater) is amply sufficient to confound us doubters. In mood and manner it is, to be sure, strikingly like "The Glass Menagerie." Indeed, the theme and even the story might be said to be the same, since both dramas are concerned with the desperate, unsuccessful effort of a female character to hang on to some kind of shabby gentility.

From Joseph Wood Krutch's column, "Drama," in The Nation, *165 (December 20, 1947): 686–87. Reprinted by permission of* The Nation.

But the new work is sure and sustained where the former was uncertain and intermittent. Gone are all the distracting bits of ineffectual preciosity, all the pseudo-poetic phrases, and all those occasions when the author seemed about to lose his grip upon the very story itself. From the moment the curtain goes up until it descends after the last act everything is perfectly in key and completely effective. The extent of Mr. Williams's range is still to be demonstrated. He may or he may not have much to say, and it is quite possible that sickness and failure are the only themes he can treat. But there is no longer any doubt of his originality, or of his power within the limits of what he has undertaken. Since 1930 only three new talents which seemed to promise much have appeared in our theater, and of Mr. Williams one must say what one said of Odets and Saroyan. Only time can tell just how far a young man who begins like this may possibly go.

Considered merely in terms of the story it had to tell, "The Glass Menagerie" was bleak enough, but the story of the new play is both bleaker and more frankly pathological. Its central figure is a young school teacher, daughter of a decayed Southern family, who has lost her job because she is—technically and not in the loose popular sense of the term—a nymphomaniac, and who has come, as the play opens, to seek refuge with a married sister in New Orleans. At the beginning we know nothing of the past of this central character, and we have nothing except a few intriguing, unexplained incongruities in her behavior to suggest that she is anything more than the shabby, desperately refined, and respectable young woman she seems to be. We share her distraction at the discovery that her sister has complacently accepted a descent into the blowsy happiness of a misalliance with a coarse, violent husband of frankly proletarian habits; and then, as the action proceeds, the dreadful truth about the heroine emerges until, in the terrible but finely conceived final scene, she begins what she believes is a flirtation with the attendant who has come to conduct her to the insane asylum. That the play is not merely the ugly, distressing, and possibly unnecessary thing which any outline must suggest is due, I suppose, in part to its sincerity, even more to the fact that the whole seems to be contemplated with genuine compassion and not, as is the case with so much modern writing about the lower depths, merely with relish. It remains, as there is no point in trying to deny, morbid enough. The mood and the atmosphere are what really count, and both are almost unrelievedly morbid, even, or perhaps especially, in those moments when a kind of grotesque comedy emerges. Yet despite the sensational quality of the story neither the atmosphere nor the mood is ever merely sensational. The author's perceptions remain subtle and delicate, and he is amazingly aware of nuances even in situations where nuance might seem to be inevitably obliterated by violence. The final impression left is, surprisingly enough, not of sensationalism but of subtlety.

Comparing, as one inevitably does, this play with its predecessor, the difference in merit between the two seems to be almost entirely the result of the author's vastly increased mastery of a method which is neither that of simple realism nor of frank fantasy. Obviously Mr. Williams is a highly subjective playwright. His stories are not told primarily either for their own sakes or in order to propound a merely rational thesis, but chiefly because they enable him to communicate emotions which have a special, personal significance. Already one begins to take it for granted that his plays will be immediately recognizable by their familiar themes and a sensibility as unique as that of a lyric poet. Yet he never quite abandons dramatic objectivity as a method. To go one step farther in the direction of subjectivity would inevitably be to reach "expressionism" or some other form of non-representational art. But though there is in the plays as written a certain haunting dream-like or rather nightmarish quality, the break with reality is never quite made, and nothing happens which might not be an actual event. Even the almost dadaist suggestion of the title is given—and more meaningfully than in the case of "The Glass Menagerie"—a rational explanation.

Though the new play is superbly directed by Elia Kazan and beautifully performed both by Jessica Tandy and by the other principal actors, the fact that the author has achieved so firm a mastery of his own technique will forestall the tendency to raise again the question so persistently raised in connection with "The Glass Menagerie"— the question, that is to say, whether or not it was the acting and the direction which "made" the play. "A Streetcar Named Desire" could easily be ruined by inadequate production. Everything in it depends upon the ability of a director and his actors to realize a subtle intention. One may even go so far as to say that if it had been given a bad performance, the spectator might easily have been misled into supposing, not that the production was bad, but that there had been nothing to produce. But to say that is by no means to say that the play was "made" by the director or the actors. It was made in the first instance by Mr. Williams himself, a playright who demands much but who gives even more.

John Mason Brown: Southern Discomfort

The sense of being familiar with the new and the strange is no uncommon experience. We have all had it. We have found ourselves in places unvisited by us before, and yet felt unaccountably at home there. We have been confident that we were looking upon a sight already seen, if not in this existence, in another. Time, like geography, has played these tricks upon us. An unconscious past has been overlaid upon a conscious present. Although this intrusion has been brought about by no wilful effort of our own, the result is an unsteady double vision. It is a vision which comes by flashes, and is made the more mysterious since it is the product of our feeling rather than our seeing.

It is precisely this mirage of familiarity which "A Streetcar Named Desire" is bound to raise in the minds of those who saw "The Glass Menagerie." Tennessee Williams's new play *is* new. No one can question that. In story, setting, incident, and some of the details of its characterizations, it is a work quite different from its predecessor. It is better, deeper, richer than was that earlier drama in which the late Laurette Taylor gave a deathless performance as a faded, frumpy, Southern belle. Yet new as it is, it is scarcely novel. Even the surprises, many and startling, which it holds more closely resemble misfortunes engulfing old friends than misadventures overtaking new people.

The reasons for this are obvious. The mood of "Streetcar" is the same as that of "The Glass Menagerie"—only more so. Once again Mr. Williams is writing of the decay of Southern gentility. Once again he is a dramatist of despair, though this time frustration has been replaced by disintegration. Once again the world into which he leads us is full of shadows. It is a place of gauzes and transparencies in which the reality is suggested rather than reproduced. Although now set in New Orleans's French Quarter instead of in one of St. Louis's poorer districts, the scene continues to be a slum. Its physical grubbiness remains a match for the emotional dilapidation of some of the characters it houses.

Mr. Williams's recurrent concern is with the misfits and the broken; with poor, self-deluded mortals who, in Emerson's phrase, are pendants to events, "only half attached, and that awkwardly," to the

"*Southern Discomfort*" *by John Mason Brown. From "Seeing Things,"* The Saturday Review, *30 (December 27, 1947): 22–24. Copyright 1947, The Saturday Review Associates, Inc. Reprinted by permission of* The Saturday Review *and the estate of John Mason Brown.*

world they live in. They are victims of the same negation as the characters in "The Glass Menagerie," and sustain themselves by identical illusions. If they lie to others, their major lie is to themselves. In this way only can they hope to make their intolerable lives tolerable. Such beauty as they know exists in their dreams. For the surroundings in which they find themselves are once again as sordid as is their own living.

Blanche Du Bois, the central figure in Mr. Williams's new play, is a schoolteacher turned whore, whose mind ultimately collapses. Though younger and far more relentlessly explored as a character, she is a kissing-cousin of the dowdy Amanda who, in "The Glass Menagerie," sustained herself by her unreliable prattle of a white-columned past. The man who falls in love with Blanche is the same Gentleman Caller with whom, in Mr. Williams's earlier script, Amanda's crippled daughter fell in love. His ingenuousness is unchanged; the childlike quality in a hulking male is no less constant. He is as surely a victim of his mother as Amanda's sailor son, in Mr. Williams's previous work, was the victim of Amanda.

Yet, in spite of these seeming duplications, "A Streetcar Named Desire" is no replica of "The Glass Menagerie." If it repeats certain patterns, it does so only to extend them. It is a maturer play; in fact, in some respects the most probing script to have been written by an American since Clifford Odets wrote "Awake and Sing."

Mr. Williams, let me quickly add, is a dramatist who has little in common with Mr. Odets except for his eye for small details and the vitality with which he can project character in the round. The proletarian protest; the flaming indignation; the awareness of how good people are thwarted and wasted; the over-easy blaming of "The System" for this; the sense of writing with a pen held in a clenched fist; the pungent, sometimes too florid, phrases; and the positive hope for the better world that might come—all these Odetsian traits are missing. Yet both writers, different as they are, are plainly men who have read Chekhov with profit and affection.

In general, Mr. Williams has more in common with William Saroyan, another good Chekhovian, than with Mr. Odets. He has something of the same enchantment; of the same lyricism; of the same reliance upon music; and of the same ability to evoke mood and transcend realism. But Mr. Saroyan's innocence; his glistening, youthful belief in man's goodness; his flagrant, unashamed sentimentality; the bluebird's song he keeps singing in the presence of pain or in the midst of misery; and his eruptive, though dangerous, talent for what amounts to written improvisation are characteristics conspicuous by their absence in Mr. Williams.

Mr. Williams is a more meticulous craftsman. His is a manifestly slower, less impromptu manner of writing. His attitude towards his people is as merciless as Mr. Saroyan's is naïve. He is without illusions. His men and women are not large-spirited and noble, or basically good. They are small and mean; above all, frustrated. He sees them as he believes they are, not as they would like to be or as he would like to have them. They have no secrets from him or from us when he is through with them. They may have little sweetness, but they are all lighted.

Mr. Williams's approach to them is as tough-minded as James M. Cain's would be. This is the more surprising, considering how Chekhovian or Saroyanesque are his moods. Indeed, there are scenes in "A Streetcar Named Desire" which suggest the most unlikely of collaborations. They sound as if Mr. Cain and Mr. Saroyan had written them jointly. For the magic one associates with Mr. Saroyan at his best is there. It is there in spite of the brutality of the action, the spiritual squalor of the heroine, the utter negation of the mood, and the sordidness of the episodes. Mr. Williams's new-old play is at once absorbing and appalling; poignant and amoral; drab and magical. Although a smear in a biological laboratory rather than "a slice of life," it has its haunting, moonlit aspects.

I doubt if any woman in any American play has been drawn more unsparingly than is Blanche Du Bois, the schoolteacher whose gradual descent into madness is followed in "A Streetcar Named Desire." Strindberg could not have been more ruthless in dealing with her selfishness. He, however, would have hated her, where Mr. Williams, without pleading for her, understands—and would have us understand—what has brought about her decline. He passes no moral judgment. He does not condemn her. He allows her to destroy herself and invites us to watch her in the process.

Mr. Williams names an outside cause for the first unhinging of her mind—the fact that Blanche's husband, whom she loved dearly, had turned out to be a homosexual. Upon her discovery of his secret he had blown out his brains. Although this outward tragedy may have damaged her reason, Mr. Williams presents it as being by no means the only tragedy of Blanche Du Bois's life. Her abiding tragedy comes neither from her family's dwindling fortunes nor from her widow's grief. It is sprung from her own nature. From her uncontrollable duplicity. From her pathetic pretensions to gentility, even when she is known as a prostitute in the little town in which she was brought up. From her love of the refined when her life is devoted to coarseness. From the fastidiousness of her tastes and the wantonness of her desires. From her incapacity to live up to her dreams. Most particularly, from her selfishness and her vanity, which are insatiable.

Those who have read Mr. Williams's script (as I have not) assure

me that, though scene after scene possesses merit, the real job of pulling
it together and transforming it into a play has been done by Elia
Kazan rather than by Mr. Williams. It is easy to believe this. Mr.
Kazan's direction throughout is brilliantly creative. His imagination is
at all times equal to Mr. Williams's. He succeeds in combining stylization with realism. He is able to capture to the full the inner no less
than the outer action of the text. He knows when to jab a climax
home, when to rely on mood, when to focus the attention pitilessly
on the principals, or when to establish in Reginald Marsh terms the
tenement atmosphere.

Jo Mielziner's share in the evening is as contributive as Mr. Kazan's.
His setting is one of the most distinguished he has designed in his
distinguished career. It consists of two dreary rooms on the first floor
of a dilapidated building in New Orleans. These are flanked on one
side by the bathroom in which Blanche takes incessant warm tubs,
and on the other by iron stairs leading up to other flats housing other
families whose lives, one gathers, are no less wretched and tumultuous.
The walls of Mr. Mielziner's tenement are transparent. Through
them the French Quarter can be seen. And in them a symbol exists
for Mr. Williams's inward and outward approach to his people.

A proof of the virtues of Mr. Williams's new play is that everyone
working upon it has been stimulated to do his best. As Blanche Du
Bois, Jessica Tandy gives a memorable performance. She does not
spare herself any more than Mr. Williams has spared his heroine.
She dodges none of the exposures of the text by playing for sympathy.
She is what Mr. Williams describes her as being. Her lies, her pathetic
ardors, her drinking, her selfishness, and the encroachments of her
madness are all clearly and unforgettably established. She has her
schoolma'am moments and her interludes of pretended gentility, both
of which are interrupted by sudden glimpses into the woman she
truly is.

As the victim of Momism Blanche almost lures into marriage, Karl
Malden suggests movingly all that is trusting, naïve, good, and slow-
witted in the character. Kim Hunter plays Blanche's self-effacing sister
with warmth and tenderness. As her Polack husband, Marlon Brando
is excellent. It is almost impossible to realize that this is the same Mr.
Brando who, not long ago, was giving so ineffectual a performance as
Marchbanks in Miss Cornell's "Candida." Where he then seemed weak
and plainly inadequate, he is now all force and fire; a Rodin model;
a young Louis Wolheim with Luther Adler's explosiveness.

Although no one is apt to describe Mr. Williams's new play as
pleasant, its power is incontestable. It could stand cutting, and certain
of its scenes, such as its final one, might be bettered by rewriting. But
both as written and as staged, one thing is certain. "A Streetcar Named

Desire" is more than a work of promise. It is an achievement of un-usual and exciting distinction.

Irwin Shaw: Masterpiece

As far as I'm concerned, even the ushers and ticket-takers at the Ethel Barrymore Theater are beautiful these nights, and the cop on the corner of Forty-seventh Street and Eighth Avenue, and his horse. Such is the effect of a magnificent play, magnificently done. The play is "A Streetcar Named Desire," by Tennessee Williams, and the pro-duction is the result of Elia Kazan's direction, Jo Mielziner's scenery and lighting and, I suppose, Irene Selznick's money, all of which have my unqualified blessing.

The play is better than Williams' other success, "The Glass Me-nagerie," because, while it has all of the tenderness, poetry, observa-tion and wit of the earlier piece, it adds the element of true tragedy to its other merits.

It is a despairing and lovely play, in which the author, in oblique parable form, says that beauty is shipwrecked on the rock of the world's vulgarity; that the most sensitive seekers after beauty are ear-liest and most bitterly broken and perverted. It is an answer, however unintended, to "Harvey" and "The Iceman Cometh," which said that Illusion provides the necessary armor behind which life can survive. "A Streetcar Named Desire" (and what a haunting, musically dis-sonant title it is) tells us that Illusion is an armor, but one which is always pierced, and in the most mortal spots.

But the parable is hidden artfully in the body of the play. While you are exposed to the magic on the Barrymore stage, you see only the suffering, doomed struggles of a lying, posing, half-demented, pathetic, fully drawn woman, whose dreams are all lace and magnolia, and whose life, given cheaply to whisky and men, has been unbeliev-ably raw and sordid. You may think, as I do, that Williams' general-ization is too easily defeatist, that he himself has dipped into the most squalid depths and come up with a steadily beautiful work of art; but, particularly, there is an awesome credibility about the character of his main creation, Blanche du Bois. She is as real to us as if she were a living woman put to the torture and done to death in our own front parlor.

The play is written with a triumphantly heightened naturalism,

"Masterpiece" by Irwin Shaw. From The New Republic, *117 (December 22, 1947): 34–35. Copyright © 1947, Harrison-Blaine of New Jersey, Inc.; used with per-mission.*

in which the rhythms and images of ordinary life are subtly combined and contrasted with a verselike elegance of phrase. It falls on the
ear like fresh rain after the businesslike tracts of manufactured dialogue which have too long done duty for human speech on the
American stage. It finally has the surprising effect of seeming infinitely
more real, more like life itself, than all the clipped banalities lesser
playwrights put together in the dreary name of realism.

The production matches the script point for point. Absolutely ar-
bitrary, with a back wall through which we can see the street beyond,
with a steel staircase spiraling off to one side, going God-knows-where,
with lights softly growing in intensity and capriciously fading off into
darkness, with a spotlight lovingly following the heroine throughout
the evening, with voices and music breaking in again and again with
no reasonable justification but thunderous effect, the director and
scene designer have boldly realized that a world on the stage has
exactly the limits, the beauty and the belief that the artist wishes
them to have.

In his direction Kazan has caught the combination of Southern,
rambling languor, slashed by moments of blazing violence, that the
play calls for. In the same way, Jo Mielziner has designed a setting
that is at once sordid, ugly, dreamlike and glorious.

Jessica Tandy, in the heroic role of Blanche, suffers only from the
fact that some seasons back we all saw Laurette Taylor in another
Williams play. Everything that talent, intelligence, discipline can do,
Miss Tandy does. We pity her, we are amused by her, we suffer with
her and are enchanted with the clarity and grace with which she
speaks her lines—and at the end, broken and bereft of reason, she
leaves us desolate. But the solitary and touching genius that was Miss
Taylor is not here. It is unjust to judge an actress by such a fanatic
standard, but it is impossible not to remember.

With his brooding, savage portrayal of the violent Stanley Kowalski,
Marlon Brando arrives as the best young actor on the American stage.
Most young men in our theater seem hardly violent enough to com-
plain to a waiter who has brought them cream instead of lemon.
Brando seems always on the verge of tearing down the proscenium
with his bare hands.

Representing the healthy, driving forces of the flesh, Brando plays
a useful trick on us. He is so amusing in a direct, almost childlike way
in the beginning, and we have been so conditioned by the modern
doctrine that what is natural is good, that we admire him and sym-
pathize with him. Then, bit by bit, with a full account of what his
good points really are, we come dimly to see that he is one of the
villains of the piece, brutish, destructive in his healthy egotism, dan-

gerous, immoral, surviving. By a slouching and apelike posture, by a curious, submerged and almost inarticulate manner of speech, by an explosive quickness of movement, Brando documents completely a terrifying characterization.

In almost every play, no matter how excellent, the author usually neglects one character. In this play it is Stella Kowalski, Blanche's sister. The idea for the character is interesting—the upper-class girl who for the overbearing pleasures of the flesh has willfully and delightedly allowed herself to become the slattern her husband can desire and understand. But in its development the character is skimped; neither the slattern nor the belle is convincing. Miss Kim Hunter, playing this troubled role, is baffled by her problem and leaves it where she found it. On almost any other stage in New York she would probably appear as a superior actress. But in this gifted company, new standards must be applied.

I must put in a word about one of my favorite actors, Karl Malden, who seems, in a wide variety of parts through the recent years, never to have been able to do any wrong. Here, as a shy, anguished, groping and disappointed suitor, he supplies a rueful humor and an elephantine delicacy that are immensely helpful.

Harold Hobson: Miss Vivien Leigh

When this play opened the pressure of other productions prevented my dealing with it adequately. Since then it has been violently condemned by many people whose opinions I respect. Its condemnation does grave harm, not least by suggesting to the salacious that it is the sort of thing they will enjoy, while discouraging serious theatregoers from seeing it. It may easily have the worst possible effect, by keeping the right audiences away from the Aldwych, and packing the wrong ones in.

"A Streetcar" has been spoken of, in the words that Clement Scott used about "Ghosts," as "a nasty and a vulgar" play. Yet it is strictly, and even puritanically, moral. It is the story of a woman, not otherwise questionable, whose sexual nature is, against the striving of better things in her, rendered so uncontrollable by circumstances that she ends in madness. It is no good saying that this kind of character is never portrayed on the stage. What we really mean is that it is never portrayed honestly. In musical comedies and farces girls who behave

"Miss Vivien Leigh" by Harold Hobson. From The Sunday Times, *London, November 13, 1949. Reprinted by permission of Times Newspapers Limited.*

like Blanche du Bois are common enough; and they end not in an
asylum, but in sables and Park Lane. They are glamorised by bright
lights, dazzling clothes and catchy songs.

Against these entertainments no protest is ever made. No one can
in general enjoy "Oklahoma!" more than I do, but I am amazed that
those who are shocked by "A Streetcar" can apparently listen to the
song "I Can't Say No" without offence. In its basic assumptions Mr.
Tennessee Williams's play, far from being daring, is rigidly, even
timidly, conventional. It never departs by a hair's breadth from its
text, which is that the wages of sin is spiritual death.

Were this all that could be said about "A Streetcar" its morality
would be impregnable, but audiences might reasonably feel that it
made too great demands upon their nerves and endurance. But it is
not all. Without compromise of principles or concession to sentimentality, Mr. Williams, looking into Blanche with inflexible judgment
but also with human pity, legitimately finds in her story many moments of touching beauty.

Blanche, driven out of her home town in poverty, comes to her
sister's slum tenement in New Orleans, and meets suspicion and hostility. At the end of the third scene of the opening act Harold Mitchell,
the best of her blustering, filthy-tempered brother-in-law's poker-playing friends, offers to light her cigarette. It is the tiniest thing in the
world, the commonest courtesy; it is also the first kindness shown to
Blanche since the curtain rises, and she almost breaks down. Anyone
who can watch this episode unmoved must be as insensitive as he is
imperceptive. But all the story of Blanche's relationship with Mitchell,
with its shy, tentative affection, its curious, sad formality, is wholly
lovely.

Blanche's character is not the stuff out of which great tragedy is
made. From the point of view of construction the play has too many
short scenes. The language is sometimes coarse, and several characters
referred to but not seen lack solidity. But the play is a distinguished
work, in its reiterated insistence upon the need for kindness, noble; it
is finely directed by Sir Laurence Olivier, and finely acted.

Mr. Bonar Colleano's Stanley Kowalski vibrates with energy: he is
the world's raw nerve, and screams at a touch. Mr. Bernard Braden,
as Mitchell, is moving in his show of simple affection: his sudden
bursts of serious, precise speaking, at once impulsive and pedantic, the
sign of youth, are oddly attractive. The best thing I saw in America
was Miss Uta Hagen's performance as Blanche: Miss Vivien Leigh's is
finer.

I saw it again on Wednesday afternoon, and found it almost unbearably poignant. I said a month ago that this performance casts out
pity with terror. I was wrong. The terror is there, and the struggle

with the woman medical attendant chills the spine. But the pity is overwhelming. Out of a score of brilliant details in Miss Leigh's performance I will mention only one: her pathetic nervous brightening at the merest suggestion of a compliment is heartrending. Pale, worn out with passion and misfortune, she drifts down her terrible path, except for a few moments of distracted hope, with a frightening, flutteringly resistant inevitability that makes her performance one of the great things of the theatre. I do not know which to admire the more, the power, the emotion, of this performance, or the courage that enables Miss Leigh to go on giving it, with undimmed lustre, amidst these foolish suggestions that her play is a public indecency.

René MacColl: Laughter dans le Tramway

Over here in Paris there has been a risible piece of entertainment on offer. No, not a new *boîte* on the Left Bank, but a smash hit in the theater, entitled *Un Tramway Nommé Désir.*

(*Do* look out for it. I'm told that you had something on Broadway bearing a faintly similar title—but that must be purely coincidental, as the saying goes; because everybody said your piece was so terribly sad and frightfully sordid. This one that I'm talking about is almost as uproarious as the Marx Brothers at their topmost peak.)

Here's what happens: the curtain rises on a scene which—if we are to believe the program—is taking place in New Orleans, Louisiana. It's supposed to be the home of a Polish–American called Stan.

One can tell at a glance that it is, *hélas,* a strictly underprivileged home, because (*a*) its walls are diaphanous, thus enabling *ces messieurs et mesdames* of the audience to see right through them into the *rue en dehors,* and (*b*) there is no sign of a video set. A telephone, yes (one of those gangling French jobs, about a foot high), but definitely no video.

Now this Stan, the Polish–American, is played—and follow this carefully, if you please—by a very good-looking and slender young Frenchman called Yves: Yves is a cross between Jean Sablon and Louis Jourdan, the juvenile lead in films. As an ape man, he looks like something dreamed up by Christian Dior. But he does have fine back muscles. He realizes this, and you get to know all those muscles like old friends before the evening is out because this Stan–Yves keeps on

"Laughter dans le Tramway" by René MacColl. From The Atlantic Monthly, *186 (July 1950): 94–95. Copyright © 1950, by The Atlantic Monthly Company, Boston, Mass. Reprinted with permission of the author and The Atlantic Monthly Company.*

changing his shirt like mad. Whenever he does so, with his back elaborately turned to the audience, a man in the wings, or possibly lying in front of the footlights, turns on a special off-mauve light which shadows up the muscles most toothsomely.

And just why does Stan change his shirt so often? Nine times out of ten it's *pour le bollinck*. (And of course you know all about *le bollinck*, don't you? Sir Francis Drake, you will recall, was engaged in *le bollinck* that time on Plymouth Ha! when the Spennish *flotte* showed up.)

Stella, the little woman, is apt to dart out at Stan. "Stan!" she cries reproachfully. "Is it that you go out of our hearth once again—to *le bollinck?*"

"Of course," returns Stan, a he–Polish–American–Frenchman to his very sideburns, flexing his back muscles, which *le bollinck* is apt to develop like the very deuce. As an afterthought he turns and hurls wifey to the floor. Never get between a Polish–American–Frenchman and his *bollinck* seems here to be the inescapable moral.

But Stan has his intellectual moments too. It's not all outdoor sports for him. Often he dons a tasty soccer jersey (daring vertical stripes) and settles down at home for a good game of *le pokkaire* with friends. But the beasts drink as they play—and that provides a rich moment of high comedy that even Groucho has rarely bettered. For the four men take turns at huge-seeming swigs from one tiny bottle of French (Pilsen type) beer.

Round and round the table of debauchees goes that sad little bottle —and in no time its innocuous contents transform the four into sententious drunks. Their eyes glaze and they give way to such unspeakable remarks as *"Zut, alors!"* and *"Et bien—toi!"*

Says the "Analysis of the Performance," thoughtfully provided at the rear of the program, "It is an earthy life this, whose unique distractions are the bowling, the poker, the cinema, and the love." Aha— the love!

Sure enough, into this uniquely earthy life there flutters a female character called Blanche du Bois. She turns out to be Stan's sister-in-law, and she looks like a fugitive from a down payment. Stan dislikes Blanche right from the start. For one thing, she puts her capacious wardrobe trunk right spang in front of the cupboard where he stores his Pernod-Viskey. Then again she always seems to be in the bathroom when he gets home all tuckered out from a hard day's work at *le bollinck*.

Blanche, let's face it, is just a touch tactless. She asks Stella: "See you in the character of that one the least trace of *un gentleman?*" Stan, on the other side of the bedroom curtain, overhears this slur. Glowering, he changes his shirt.

Every so often Stan, to prove that he is indeed no gentleman (pronounced throughout this offering as "jantlaman"), has a crack at the fourth of the distractions listed in the "Analysis of the Performance." You can always tell that something is brewing because—you've guessed it—off comes another shirt. However, the subtle French prefer to leave nothing to chance. They call in *le symbolisme* to aid *l'amour*. Stan does three mad *entrechats* across the stage, wearing a pair of bright red silk pajama trousers, but with bared torso-back strictly audiencewards. Blanche glances up from her dreams of *la plantation*, startled. *"Brute, va!"* she ejaculates. Black-out.

But immediately, through the diaphanous walls, you can perceive, in the street outside, a colored shimmy dancer billowing around to the sound of voodoo drums. The audience is notably entranced by this conceit. *"Ah, ces Américains!"* they observe knowingly to one another.

The shimmy dancer is quickly succeeded by a really typical American street vendor. A character wearing a hard straw hat, horn-rimmed glasses, and spats is next seen outside.

"Ertdergs, ertdergs," he drones. The audience instantly catches on. (And you must know all about ertdergs, don't you? They *mangent* them at *le bessboll game*.)

So it goes. Never a dull moment. "I permit myself to draw attention to a certain lack of manners," says one character. "He is frankly bestial!" snaps another, in the authentic accents of Louisiana.

The straight man is called Meetch. He wears plastic suspenders and wants to introduce Blanche to his *maman*. But Stan cannot forgive the difficulties about getting a bath in his own *salle de bain*. He strides in suddenly, *très brute*, past the bespatted ertderg men outside. He is wearing a steamer cap, windbreaker jacket, plus-four trouserings, and white socks. Caddishly enough, he informs Meetch that it is by no means only a down payment that Blanche is a fugitive from. Meetch instantly feels that *Maman* wouldn't much care for anything like that. Pausing only to toss off half a glass of beer, he leaves the stage with unsteady gait.

Back to the "Analysis of the Performance":—

"Blanche, beneath this final stroke of fate, feels her reason vacillate." But the blow only makes her the more talkative. There is no holding her now.

And obviously there's only one remedy. Yes, the Great American Remedy: call in the psychiatrist. But lucky Blanche! She, it seems, is to get him free, instead of having to shell out the 25-dollar fee twice weekly, which is what the run-of-the mill patient would do.

So, in a surprise ending, Blanche neatly turns the tables on Stan-le-Brute, Meetch-le-Milksop, Stella-la-Femme, the card players, shimmy dancers, and ertderg men. For, like all good *Américains*—even the most underprivileged—they have all been longing to be vetted by a good psychiatrist. And now here is tiresome old Blanche pulling it off ahead of them all—and for free.

And as she sweeps out in triumph, arm in arm with Monsieur le Directeur du Snake-Pit, all hands burst into tears of jealous rage and maudlin self-pity.

Rideau.

Don't miss this if you can catch it on the road. One long laugh. Guaranteed to help you forget your own troubles for a couple of hours.

PART TWO

The Play as Dramatic Literature

Williams' Feminine Characters

by Durant da Ponte

It is in his ability to create striking feminine portraits, however, that Mr. Williams truly excels. This is no mean distinction. Consider in the history of fiction and the stage how rarely vital, rounded female figures appear. Some of Shakespeare's heroines, Becky Sharpe, Emma Bovary, Anna Karenina, possibly Molly Bloom, perhaps Hedda Gabler, —there are not many who tower above their sisters to achieve the rarefied air of absolute greatness. Edmund Fuller accounts for this circumstance on the grounds that women have traditionally been accorded a subservient and secondary role in society, and even in a more enlightened age like our own certain doubts and ambiguities exist concerning just what is or should be their rightful position.

In Tennessee Williams' case, the picture is further complicated by the fact that many of his women have been created in and are forced to operate within a particular framework—namely, the American South, both as it is and as it once was. There thus tends to be established a stereotype—let us call it the faded Southern belle—but it is a stereotype with a difference. There have been, of course, Southern belles in literature before—faded and even jaded. But there have not been many like Amanda and Laura Wingfield, Alma Winemiller, or Blanche DuBois. It is with these that a study of Tennessee Williams' women must logically begin.

Mr. Williams once described himself as "an old-fashioned romanticist," a bit of self-characterization that would doubtless come as something of a surprise to such old-fashioned romanticists as Thomas Nelson Page and James Lane Allen. And yet, analysis of his plays does actually reveal a certain romantic outlook, if by romantic we mean yearning backwards in time to a world where ideals of gentility and

gentleness were cherished and defended. This notion is further but-
tressed by a statement the playwright made in an interview several
years ago. "I'm a compulsive writer," Mr. Williams explained, "because what I am doing is creating imaginary worlds into which I can
retreat from the real world because . . . I've never made any kind
of adjustment to the real world."

Here quite clearly is a major clue to an understanding both of the
playwright and his characters. Many of the personages he has created
would seem to be projections of his own disoriented personality,
frightened, timid, groping, highly sensitive, somewhat neurotic
dreamers who, like their creator, are unable to adjust to the harsh
realities of a world of crass materialism and brute strength. Or, if
they have been forced to make an adjustment, this adjustment usually
hardens and distorts them, as in the case of Amanda in *The Glass
Menagerie*. For certainly in many ways Amanda *has* come to terms
with the real world (although in many other ways she has not). . . .

If we did not laugh at Amanda, I suspect we should cry, for there
is a certain pathetic heroism in her efforts to provide for her children
—her daughter, especially. A measure of her refusal to face actuality
appears in her attitude toward Laura—the cotton wads she makes her
stuff into her blouse ("gay deceivers" she calls them); her shrill denial
that Laura is crippled: "Don't say crippled! You know that I never
allow that word to be used!" Amanda is a curious combination of
exaggerated gentility on one hand and exasperating practicality on
the other. "You be the lady this time and I'll be the darky," she tells
Laura at the dinner table. "Resume your seat, little sister—I want
you to stay fresh and pretty—for gentlemen callers." And to Tom:
". . . chew—chew! Eat food leisurely, son, and really enjoy it . . .
chew your food and give your salivary glands a chance to function!"
At times cranky and cantankerous, at times wistful and tender, at
times gallant and heroic—Amanda is one of Tennessee Williams'
most impressive creations.

The problem of withdrawal from reality and ultimate retreat into
the private world of insanity is best illustrated in the character of
Blanche duBois, the memorable and tragic heroine of *A Streetcar
Named Desire*. In this portrayal we find an interesting illustration of
some of Mr. Williams' major concerns (notably the faded Southern
belle unable to adjust to a hostile environment) and also of his characteristic method (a calculated ambiguity in presenting his material).

The playwright makes use of an ironic name symbolism in connection with the two sisters around whom the action of the play revolves.
Blanche and Stella may at one time in the past have been appropriately

designated by "white" and "star," but when we see them during the course of the play, the character of Blanche has become decidedly sullied and blackened, while Stella, far from aspiring like a star, has settled for an altogether earthy existence with a man who typifies basic, crude, primitive sexuality. Stanley Kowalski turns out to be Blanche's natural enemy and ultimate nemesis. It is he who delivers the *coup de grace,* although the decline of Blanche had been a long time coming. It was "All of those deaths," she tells Stella, explaining how Belle Reve (Beautiful Dream), their plantation home in Laurel, Mississippi, slipped through her fingers and was lost. There was the matter of her early marriage to an unfortunate youth who turned out to be a homosexual and who killed himself when she learned of his condition. The search for love and security in a hostile world turned Blanche eventually into a nymphomaniac. Death and desire followed one another with shattering rapidity. Blanche answered the midnight calls of soldiers passing the plantation. Soon her name became a byword in the town. Eventually she seduced a seventeen-year-old pupil in her English class and was asked to leave Laurel.

All this was in the past. When we see her during the action of the play, she retains the aura of elegance and gentility that had been her birthright. But gradually she reveals herself as already well advanced into the shadowy world of illusion. She is under the impression that an old admirer is going to invite her on a cruise, and this mythical person's presence lurks in the background as her last refuge. To Mitch, the young man who, it develops, is almost as unable to face reality as Blanche, she remarks: "I don't want realism. . . . I'll tell you what I want. Magic! Yes, yes, magic! I try to give that to people. I misrepresent things to them. I don't tell the truth. I tell what *ought* to be truth. And if that is sinful, then let me be damned for it!"

And damned, of course, Blanche is. Mr. Williams, in his characterization, is quite clear about the kind of person she has become. Everything Stanley has uncovered about her lurid past in Laurel is true. We see her taunt Mitch, making crude sport of his innocence. When she learns that he does not understand French, she toys with him: "Voulez-vous couchez avec moi ce soir? Vous ne comprenez pas? Ah, quel dommage!—I mean it's a damned good thing. . . ." Her inability to keep her hands off the young paper boy, while making for a most sensitive and touching scene, is nevertheless symptomatic. Further, she announces that she has been flirting with Stanley (and her attitude toward him is, in point of fact, curiously ambiguous). In the climactic scene, in which Stanley rapes Blanche, he recognizes the inevitability of their encounter. As he carries her inert figure to the bed, he says: "We've had this date with each other from the beginning." The result of this encounter is that Blanche's reason snaps. When we last see her, she is being led off to an asylum, now totally unable to distinguish between illusion and reality, giving herself over to the care of the doctor with a childlike simplicity and confidence and the utterance of a farewell line that has become memorable in the modern theatre: "Whoever you are—I have always depended on the kindness of strangers."

The facts here are obvious enough; but what are we to make of them? What is Mr. Williams trying to tell us? Where do his sympathies lie? Where, logically, ought ours lie? These, it seems to me, are some provocative and rather important questions posed by this admittedly greatest of all Tennessee Williams' plays. The dramatist himself (in one of his several statements of his aims as a writer) has given a partial answer. Replying to the charge that he fills his plays with "sordid characters," he stated: "I don't think Blanche DuBois was sordid. I think she was rather noble. I don't think deeply troubled people are sordid."

Certainly Blanche is "deeply troubled." Whether her behavior can be defended is another matter. At any rate, if we feel she is worth bothering with, we must attempt to understand why she acts the way she does; we must try to appreciate what has happened to her—in a general rather than in a specific sense. In so doing, we will be led to one of the themes of the play, which, briefly stated, is this: In *A Streetcar Named Desire* the dramatist is attacking those disruptive forces in modern life that have shattered traditional values and have rendered obsolete the older civilized refinements. In the face of a rising barbarism (symbolized by Stanley Kowalski), clinging to antiquated ideals, blindly groping for security in a world of chaos and flux, the gentle and basically decent Blanche can no longer find her way. She is ultimately lost and thus becomes a fit subject for a modern tragedy. Our sympathies, it seems to me, must clearly be with her rather than with her sister, who has capitulated, who has joined the enemy. The play thus becomes a sort of commentary on modern life, brilliantly elucidated through the manipulation of a psychologically sound (in the best Freudian sense) group of character symbols.

A Trio of Tennessee Williams' Heroines:
The Psychology of Prostitution

by Philip Weissman

In the early 1940's, a young playwright appeared on the scene with acclaimed creative gifts, particularly for the portrayal of psychopathological character. Thus in this period the world became familiar with Tennessee Williams' play *The Glass Menagerie* and shortly thereafter with the now-famous character portrayal of Blanche DuBois in *A Streetcar Named Desire*.

In 1942, a man of the theater and arts made public Freud's hitherto unknown and unpublished paper, "Psychopathological Characters on Stage," which was written in 1904. In an accompanying essay, Max Graf wrote: "Freud gave it [the paper] to me, and I now submit it to a world in which the ideas of Freud have become part of the spiritual air we breathe."

In this early study, Freud recommends that the character in psychopathological dramas reveals in an ambiguous form the struggle of unconscious impulses toward consciousness. He emphasizes the essential nature of ambiguity in this art form. Kris and Kaplan (1952), expanding on Empsom's essay (1931) on ambiguity in poetic language, develop the conception of art "as a process of communication and re-creation in which ambiguity plays a central role." Thus we have brought together analytic observations on psychopathological drama, on the use of poetic language, and on art in general. This may be particularly fruitful here, since Tennessee Williams is both poet and dramatist. His plays, even when not written in verse, are regarded as essentially approaches to character by way of poetic revelation. Intending to focus on his character creations, we are suddenly and simultaneously struck by the superimposed impressions and implications of his

"A Trio of Tennessee Williams' Heroines: The Psychology of Prostitution" (*excerpts*). *From Philip Weissman,* Creativity in the Theater (*New York: Basic Books, Inc., Publishers, 1965*). *Originally published as "Psychopathological Characters in Current Drama: A Study of a Trio of Heroines,"* in American Imago, *17* (*Fall 1960*): *271–88. Reprinted by permission of Basic Books, Inc. and* American Imago.

poetic language. It is self-evident that his poetic dramas express higher
levels of artistic creation.

One distinction from the current breed of dramatists of psychopathology to be noted in Williams is his uncompromising complete-
ness of portrayal. Williams' characters are not always favorably responded to by audiences.[1] However, there is rarely a lack of emotional
response in either his critics or supporters. There is also rarely a moment in the unfolding of his plays in which one is not "in the grip of
his emotions, rather than capable of rational judgment."[2] If our
dramatists of today would heed the requisites suggested by Freud sixty
years ago, the goal of true artistic achievement would be much closer
for them.

We are indebted to Williams for a most unusual portrayal of a
thirteen-year-old girl from a small Mississippi town who is a juvenile
derelict. In this one-act play, *This Property Is Condemned,* the young
girl, Willie, is seen living secretively alone in her condemned house,
which her mother deserted by running off with a railroad man, one
of the many who frequented her combined home and house of prostitution. The prostitutes had been Willie's mother and her idolized
older sister Alva. Her alcoholic father disappeared shortly after the
mother. Willie lived with Alva until Alva developed tuberculosis and
died.

Thus, Willie sees the life of her dead sister Alva as a success story
studded with scenes of many admirers who showered her with gifts.
It is to be noted in Williams' characterization of deserted or deprived
or depraved heroines that they seek both solace and sanction in
fantasies that reconstruct their current or former activities into the
ideal of the pretty Southern belle who has many young, handsome, and
wealthy admirers. Likewise, in *Hello from Bertha,* the prostitute
Bertha, who is suffering from a venereal tubal infection, clings to the
memory of her affair with Charlie Aldrich, the hardware man from
Memphis, with a fantasy in which he is an ever-loving figure who will
rescue her from her plight. In *The Lady of Larkspur Lotion,* the
bleached-blonde, forty-year-old, alcoholically delusioned prostitute who
calls herself Mrs. Hardwick–Moore cannot pay her room rent in the
French Quarter. Defensively and delusionally, she demands that her

[1] Perhaps this can be compared to the way the general public only likes and in
some cases only understands a mild caricature of psychoanalysis and often shows
its unhidden hostility and open fears of its real representation.

[2] In his paper, Freud (1942, p. 463) comments on the psychopathological drama
as follows: "It appears to be one of the prerequisites of this art form that the
struggle of the repressed impulse to become conscious, recognizable though it is,
is so little given a definite name that the process of reaching consciousness goes on
in turn within the spectator while his attention is distracted and he is in the grip
of his emotions, rather than capable of rational judgment."

landlady rid the place of roaches and haughtily explains that there has been a delay in the quarterly payment which she regularly receives from the man who takes care of her Brazilian rubber plantation.

Running through the heroines of Williams' plays, the mixture of prostitute and prostitute fantasy is always present with artistic ambiguity, as are pride and poverty, social achievement and ostracism, and, finally, reality and fantasy. In Williams' plays, one is impressed with the thorough integrative ambiguity and the similar thoroughness of stringencies elaborated in the depiction of his psychopathological heroines.[3] Thus, Blanche DuBois is constantly contained in a portrayal of an exhibitionistic woman concerned with her appearance and clothes and with when she is seen and not seen. The heroine here is at each moment entrenched in the eyes of the author, the other actors, herself, and the audience as a woman who encompasses every variation and vicissitude of the fears and wishes of being looked at. To be looked at in admiration of beauty, in despair of waning youth, in the brutality of daylight, in the kindliness of night, or in the evanescence of cheap costume jewelry and summer frock is to be Blanche DuBois.

Beyond this clear-cut exhibitionist identity of Blanche DuBois, which makes her always believable and enactable, we must seek out Blanche in the deepest depiction of her inner conflicts, of her failing social adjustment, and of her final tragedy. Williams' heroines frequently meet the poignant pressure of unconscious strivings and catastrophic realities with a delusional denial of reality, as is demonstrated by the *Larkspur Lotion* heroine who awaits the harvest of her Brazilian rubber plantation. The characters' delusional denials become a part of Williams' inspirational point of departure as they regress into created fantasies of poetic ambiguity that are either spoken or enacted. His characters weave fantasies that unburden the momentary crisis, transform narcissistic injury into painless gratification, and devise schemes of secure eternities.

But what are Blanche DuBois' repressed wishes, struggles of conscience, and ego-ideals? What is her total adaptive adjustment? Where does she fit in our frail schemes which separate neurosis from psychosis? Is her prostitutional psychopathy immoral, amoral, or asocial? Williams approaches these questions in his stage direction when he refers to her as a neurasthenic personality. How much beyond Williams' own description we can carry this is a question.

Let us for the moment attempt to "psychoanalyze" Blanche DuBois

[3] It is noteworthy that actresses who have played Williams' heroines have often transformed their latent talents into performances of great achievement and recognition. In many cases, the already-accomplished actress seems to have added immeasurably to her status in the role of a Williams heroine.

and account for her promiscuous quasi-prostitutional life. Following
the direction of the drama's plot, we might conclude that Blanche
DuBois has unresolved oedipal wishes which culminate in her enactment of a single impulsive relationship with her brother-in-law Stanley
and subsequently results in her complete breakdown and abandonment as punishment for the direct fulfillment of this wish. We could
then account for her promiscuity as disguised but consciously enacted
repetitions of the same wish. We could also state that her early, short-
lived tragic marriage to a suicidal homosexual and her desperate at-
tempts to retain the family plantation (which she states was ruined
"as piece by piece our improvident grandfathers and father and uncles
and brothers exchanged the land for their epic fornications—to put
it plainly"), and finally her inability to subsequently undertake a
functioning marriage as did her sister Stella—all these facts seem further variations of her unresolved oedipal situation. We might also
conclude that sexual maturity (genitality) has been surrendered and
reduced to exhibitionism and promiscuity, which became the regressed
functioning levels of her sexual gratification.

But the methodology employed in the analysis of a created character cannot be so satisfactory as when employed in clinical psychoanalysis. For one thing, we cannot ask these characters or even the
author to free-associate. Nor can we remove their resistances and ana-
lyze their defenses, dreams, and fantasies. There is no next moment
when more of the unconscious can then be made available. We also
have to deal with the limited historical material that the author has
made available to us in a single session. It is particularly interesting
that Williams' characters never relate much of their early childhood.
Their lives seem to begin for them mainly in early adolescence, more
rarely in puberty. The contents of infancy and latency are well sealed.
This effective omission of their early childhood may have a strong
correlation with the credibility of their dramatic and colorful episodes
of acting out.

Another difficulty confronting the analyst trying to "psychoanalyze"
the created character is that the usual procedure tends to reduce the
creation to a more-or-less single ambiguity. This is redundant to the
essence of creativity, which, according to Kris, should be a cluster of
multiple integrative ambiguities. We must bear in mind that the attempt to reduce creative material which shows preconscious elements
to a specific unconscious meaning is to partake of the responses of
any ordinary member of an audience who comes away from an artistic creation with only a "personal" message.

Since "psychoanalyzing" Blanche DuBois offers only incomplete
solutions to the understanding of her psychopathological character, an

alternative methodological approach suggests itself. Since a created character originally belongs to the inspired ego of the author, we might examine other inspirational emanations (in this case, other characters from other plays) and search for common unconscious denominators. We have already demonstrated that Blanche of *A Streetcar Named Desire* has in common with the girl Willie of *This Property Is Condemned* and Mrs. Hardwick–Moore of *The Lady of Larkspur Lotion* an identical major defense mechanism—the delusional denial of reality and of inner conflicts. This hints at the idea that little Willie, Blanche, and Mrs. Hardwick–Moore are derivatives of a single image in the author's unconscious.

We note that our trio of heroines has further in common complete abandonment by friends and family; all three are equally preoccupied and confronted with their lost home and property. For the little girl Willie, it is her condemned home to which she clings desperately; for Blanche, it is the lost battle for her plantation called Belle Reve; and, for the deluded, disoriented Mrs. Hardwick–Moore, it is her Brazilian rubber plantation which is a mile from the Mediterranean and from which, on a clear day, it is possible to distinguish the white chalk cliffs of Dover—to this delusional home she adheres with the greatest tenacity.

To the growing bond of our trio, we might add the mutuality of their promiscuity and prostitution. To Willie, the future of having many gentlemen callers who will wine her, dine her, and be with her through the night is the heritage from her sister Alva. . . .

To the *Larkspur Lotion* lady, prostitution is a long-established profession. She deludes herself into the identity of a titled lady with a second-hand coat of arms who denies that she has male visitors with whom she quarrels over money for her services. Finally, our three heroines have a common fantasy of being rescued by the well-to-do admirer. For Willie, it is the freight superintendent, Mr. Johnson, "the most important character we ever had in our rooming house," with whom she goes steady and who buys her fancy shoes and corsages and takes her dancing every night. For Blanche DuBois, it is Shep Huntleigh, the college boyfriend—now an owner of oil wells in Texas —who at the height of her breakdown and homelessness she fantasies has come to rescue her. For Mrs. Hardwick–Moore, the imaginary rescuer is the rubber king from the plantation.

With only the minimal sacrifice of creative reality, it is possible to see the thirteen-year-old Willie grown into the thirty-year-old Blanche DuBois, whom we have most recently seen ejected from her last refuge and institutionalized, emerging in a final scene of deterioration and hopelessness ten years later and older as Mrs. Hardwick–Moore, whose

Belle Reve plantation becomes a Brazilian rubber plantation, whose oil king becomes a rubber king, and for whom prostitution has become a dismal reality.

Psychoanalytic literature also tends to coalesce its understanding of promiscuity and fantasies of prostitution.[4] Prostitution itself—as an institution, so to speak—has not been commented on. However, it could be said that, since fantasies are often enacted, we would find among prostitutes some who are enacting that which belongs to fantasy life. It is not assumed that all prostitutes arrive at this occupation via their fantasy lives. Environmental, cultural, and economic factors play important roles. . . .

. . . What have we learned by "psychoanalyzing" Blanche DuBois —the school teacher who has struggled unsuccessfully to maintain her family estate and has been evicted from her profession and community and finds her last refuge in the home of a younger sister's husband with whom she has an affair which terminates in her complete breakdown? From this history, we reached conclusions about Blanche's unresolved oedipal situation. Her promiscuity represents an intense expression of her unresolved oedipal wishes with disguised, unconscious incestuous objects. Her regression to exhibitionism also enables her to enact oedipal wishes by means of a regressive instinctual displacement. Her fantasies of being rescued represent the wish for a powerful but desexualized father. But, not unlike our experience in clinical analysis, the presence of the ubiquitous and often pathological oedipal solution is not always the only problem or the essential therapeutic solution for any given individual.

The second methodological approach seems the more helpful in understanding the origins of our heroine's plight. More can be learned about Blanche DuBois by studying her characteristics and problems in common with those of Willie of *This Property Is Condemned* and Mrs. Hardwick–Moore of *The Lady of Larkspur Lotion*.[5] The simultaneous study of the three heroines enables us to conclude that Blanche DuBois' fear of loneliness and abandonment is probably based on a disturbance of early object relationship, in which she differs intensely from her sister Stella. This accounts for her incapacity to establish a permanent object relationship; for that matter, every re-

[4] In analytic literature, promiscuity and prostitution are said to be related to early or severely repressed penis-envy, which gives rise to character traits of masculinity or vengeance toward men. Both traits give rise to fantasies of prostitution, and the vengeful type is related to promiscuity (Abraham, 1927).

[5] On this score, Beres (1959) states "that a person reveals himself by the choice of language, by recurrent phrases, metaphors, images or themes, is a recognized fact in psychoanalytic practice and has also been noted by literary scholars."

lationship is but a transient negation in her search for an unattainable reunion with the preoedipal mother. Her promiscuity, her unending fantasies of being rescued, and the inevitability of her final failure are further evidence of this state of affairs. The direction of Williams' plots are neither unique nor original. The story is but the vehicle for the poetic, dramatic, and deeper unconscious communication. In these aspects of his portrayals, Williams communicates to us the repetitive and overdetermined message of his unconsciously derived creation of prostitute- and prostitutelike-heroines.

Agoston's (1948) study of psychological aspects of prostitution reveals some interesting correlation between our applied studies and his observations. He describes the pseudopersonality of the prostitute, which involves the denial of identity to escape her feelings of guilt. This is extended into telling fictitious personal tales. Helene Deutsch (1948) has pointed out the convincing "pseudologia" of her prostitute patient, Anna. One can readily recall the dramatic delusional denials of Willie, Blanche, and Mrs. Hardwick–Moore. Agoston then points out that, in all cases, there is an unresolved Oedipus complex and a "complete emotional rejection by both parents, usually in actual fact, with a partial element of fantasy." [6]

Our study of Blanche's story through the plot of the play clearly demonstrated the unresolved oedipal situation and the regression to exhibitionism. The study of the triad of prostitutional heroines through their introspective and self-descriptive utterances illustrates, not only regression and the rejection by parents, but the additional disturbance in object relationships with the concomitant fears of abandonment and the restitutional fantasies of being rescued by men— which represents being reunited with the preoedipal mother. Thus our investigation of Williams' heroines tends, not only to confirm previous clinical findings in the psychology of prostitutes, but also to extend the understanding into more basic aspects of ego-development and the nature of the object relationships in such cases. Accordingly, our two methodological approaches—the comprehending of the events in the plays and studying of the fusion of the author's identical characters—give us both a longitudinal and dynamic perspective in our analytic evaluation.

It would be circumspect and limited to view Williams' *A Streetcar Named Desire* and indeed the other plays mentioned as exclusively psychopathological dramas. Freud, in his 1904 paper, classified drama into religious, character, social, psychological, and psychopathological categories. He writes: "Every combination of this situation with that

---

[6] Concomitantly, according to Agoston there is pseudo-regression to the oral/anal level in the guise of money-madness which conceals regression to the completely infantile level of exhibitionism, scopophilia, and enjoyment of magical power.

in the earlier types of drama, that is the social and the character drama, is of course possible insofar as social institutions evoke just such an inner conflict, and so on" (p. 462). Thus Blanche DuBois' struggle against Stanley and the social community becomes in addition the enactment of a character drama and a social tragedy.

Like other artists, Williams may be able to evoke the primary process and a controlled ego-regression for the purpose of creative writing, but he is bound by the unconsciously determined nature of his characterizations.[7] Perhaps, with such unconscious images, Williams is constricted to the helpless future of continuing to write tragedies about psychopathological characters, which the public may or may not like.

It is my impression that Williams' creative talent has directed itself to an overdetermined path of portraying psychopathological characters. To substantiate such an impression, a psychobiographical study of him would be necessary. The superior quality of Tennessee Williams' creations are of direct interest to us as students of mental illness. They may provide us with ways and means of analytically understanding a commonly misunderstood type of psychopathology which is rarely seen on the analyst's couch.

[7] Only in that way can Freud's requisite of the obscure revelation of the repressed impulse and Kris's requisite of aesthetic ambiguity be met.

Tennessee Williams and the
Tragedy of Sensitivity

by John T. von Szeliski

With reason, critics of the modern theatre have always complained of the weakness of modern tragedy and now, with the last O'Neill play produced and Williams and Miller obviously past their prime, they could note that entries will be few even as would-be tragedy. This weakness or absence of tragedy, I think, can largely be blamed on our playwrights' imperfect tragic vision—a lack of perspective on what they find tragic in this world. This condition is illustrated in the types of tragedy or pseudo-tragedy modern playwrights create. We have had tragedies of martyrdom, such as *Winterset* and many other Maxwell Anderson plays, wherein a death wish is supposed to be more sensible than any struggle against the tragic obstacle; tragedies of inheritance, such as *A Long Day's Journey into Night,* wherein the characters are anti-heroically trapped in a conviction that life is a treadmill of inherited guilt and sin whose rhythm cannot be altered by will; and tragedies of illusory identity—from O'Neill's *Beyond the Horizon* to Odets' *Golden Boy* and Tennessee Williams' *Sweet Bird of Youth*—in which the protagonists live disastrous lies of hopeless conflict between the real self and the idealized self. Of course, in all of these types of tragedy, what happens is not so different from the action of old, successful classics—it is instead a question of the author's own dejection about the possibility of life affirmation.

One of the most-used modes of misconceived tragic philosophy, especially in the modern American theatre, has been what I call the "tragedy of sensitivity." The over-sensitive protagonist is bound to suffer, according to this tragic vision, because the rest of the world is so insensitive. The resulting disorientation forces him to live a life which is in constant conflict with the animalism of the majority. Neurosis is the minimum result, and more often this conflict produces

"Tennessee Williams and the Tragedy of Sensitivity" by John von Szeliski. From Western Humanities Review, 20 (Summer 1966): 203–11. *Reprinted by permission of the author and* Western Humanities Review.

psychosis. The only adjustment that the deranged hero can offer is a pathetic and disastrous role-playing which to him preserves the illusions he prefers as values, but which in reality are long-dead in the ruthlessly changing world. The role-playing in this type of tragedy is dangerous in terms of the situation with which the protagonist is faced, but its most serious conflict with the life he is forced to confront is in the disorientation of the senses—chiefly esthetic and sexual sensitivity.

Either hyper-sensitivity, by contrast, serves to make the character suspect in a society which has become crudely jaded, or so the playwright shows us, and which lives life as an animal struggle and as a ritual of bestial expression and gratification. An alternative is to seek out equally disoriented souls and be confined with them in a den of despair such as that in *The Iceman Cometh*. At any rate, the values are upside down, but those who realize this are in the minority and cannot be heard. The protagonist's implied pleas, "Where am I?" and "Who am I?," are asked in a sensual context.

Outstandingly, Tennessee Williams is the spokesman of this version of hopelessness, and *A Streetcar Named Desire* most notably exemplifies the characteristics of this tragedy of disorientation-through-sensitivity. . . .

Williams probably has no plays left in him much beyond the level of the current *Slapstick Tragedy,* and our playwrights who carry on do not demonstrate that they will outgrow his vision—that of a subschool of the tragedy of sensitivity, within the larger despondency of nearly all our playwrights. The question in this article is why such "tragedy" fails.

Tennessee Williams' pessimism involves an eloquent doubt about the outcome of the constant duel between bestiality and sensitivity in the human animal. As he sees it, the coarse violators invariably conquer the delicately aware, and therefore violable, souls.

Williams says that the theme of *A Streetcar Named Desire* is that "the apes will inherit the earth." This variation of Maxwell Anderson's expression of human destiny ("The rats will inherit the earth") emphasizes a vision of man's anthropological regression. Animalism and sensuality are seen as throttling reason, compassion, and morality. Williams' sensitive protagonists cannot make successful adjustments to this kind of life-problem without becoming animals themselves. Failing this, they are destroyed. Finding most men savage, Williams' sympathy is on the side of the delicately built person whose soul is revolted by crass life. *A Streetcar Named Desire* is his allegorical demonstration of this "pitiful" situation. The wistful gentility of the Southern aristocratic tradition that lives in Blanche DuBois until the moment Stanley Kowalski violates her is weak, archaic, and impractical, and in Blanche it is a veneer for a destructive delusion, but it is vastly more humane than the animalism personified by Kowalski. It is thus also a variant of O'Neill's idea of the sensitive young poet lost in the hedonistic jungle.

Williams is a pessimist, and his own life is extremely pertinent to *A Streetcar Named Desire*. The reason for his writing is one manifestation of that pessimism, for literary creation is for him partly a psychological retreat:

> At the age of fourteen, I discovered writing as an escape from a world of reality in which I felt acutely uncomfortable. It immediately became my place of retreat, my cave, my refuge. From what? From being called a sissy by the neighborhood kids, and Miss Nancy by my father, because I would rather read books . . . than play marbles and baseball and other normal kid games.[1]

This revelation helps to support the criticism, to which Williams is open, that some of his writing is only a personal justification of his retreat or an explanation of his extreme delicacy.

The more apparent facet of his pessimism is his dark view of the world. It is based on personal hurt and a recognition of the inhuman contrast between those who are trampled to the ground and those who are allowed to survive after reality has struck its blow. . . . A hasty conclusion that might be drawn from this is that Williams lacks the objectivity to write real tragedy. The conclusion is valid only as it appears in his plays, if his psychological infirmity labors points relevant to his own torture and not to the experience of his audience. An analysis of *A Streetcar Named Desire*, however, does show that his perspective is not serene enough to fully understand his more *normal* characters and thus is less able to establish the *tragic* contrast between normal and abnormal.

Furthermore, the basic dramatic action in most of Williams' work is not the intellectual and rational one that might allow communication and friendship. Instead, the action is sexual. In the world of *A Streetcar Named Desire*, the central problem involves an inability to communicate. The author calls it a "tragedy of incomprehension." The only communication and comprehension is in sex, and the survivors are the sexually, albeit bestially, adjusted ones.

Showing a practice of sexuality that is only a substitute for love, the play is limited to dramatizing one facet of the failure of higher understanding in the world more than stimulating such understanding. Although he can show us how not to live, his pessimism does not

[1] Quoted in Randolph Goodman, *Drama on Stage* (New York, 1961), p. 274.

equip him for displaying an ideal of life, which is a product of tragedy. Herbert Muller, in *The Spirit of Tragedy,* writes:

> His tragic theme is the disorder due to sex; the implication is Lawrence's
> idea that the restoration of sexual order is the key to salvation or
> peace. His plays have . . . no wider or deeper tragic import.[2]

We can give Williams a little more than this, however; he does succeed in making such poetic use of his sensual symbols that his situations have broader, if not tragic, implications than the criticism suggests.

II

Returning to the philosophical implications of Williams' work,
his message is not a hopeful one. If the rich spirit of communication
is lacking and animalism is offered in its place, the result is a mean-
ingless existence. Insisting on some evidence of happiness on earth
instead of depending on a religious faith in some later reward, Williams cannot find real meaning in existence:

> There is a horror in things, a horror at heart of the meaninglessness
> of existence. Some people cling to a certain philosophy that is handed
> down to them and which they accept. Life has a meaning if you're
> bucking for heaven. But if heaven is a fantasy, we are in this jungle
> with whatever we can work out for ourselves. It seems to me that the
> cards are stacked against us.[3]

Because this statement of Williams' is also the view of his plays,
his plea for meeting and knowing people all over the world notwithstanding, Williams heads a theatre of hopelessness. This theatre shows
man as the perennial victim, fodder for the lower forms of human life,
and lost in his own psychological wilderness. Or, as Williams expresses
the last feature: "Hell is yourself." [4] He believes that we live in a
basically deterministic universe. He says he finds no villains or heroes
in life because evil comes and goes at its own will. Most of all, he
does not reveal a view of man as equipped to lift himself out of hell
on earth.

Yet the thing that keeps Williams from producing hopelessly depressing plays at the same time that he depicts the hopeless conclusions
of his stories is his high humane sense, and the poetry which displays
it. No matter how heavily Williams' symbols rain down upon the

---

[2] Herbert J. Muller, *The Spirit of Tragedy* (New York, 1956), p. 318.
[3] Tennessee Williams, "The Angel of the Odd," *Time,* March 9, 1962, p. 53.
[4] "The Angel of the Odd," p. 53.

audience, one must grant that he knows what is and is not humane—at least with regard to sex and related human communication. Paradoxically, his violent pictures of eroticism, bestiality, and moral degeneracy are flooded with a poetry which shows, by contrast, that to be humane is to be considerate and sensitive. He finds hopelessness in not caring and, while he goes ahead to prove in his plays that most people do *not* care, the fact that the poet cares infuses his work with values. Some of these are unorthodox, but they are values all the same.

One might expect to take this for granted in an artist, but it is not common in the modern drama. Esteemed playwrights such as Arthur Miller and Eugene O'Neill can dramatize evil and ask questions and request attention for those unable to speak for themselves, but they do not really contribute their own values to the display or answer their own questions. There are no solutions to the problems in Williams' plays either, but at least it is clear what Williams regards as inhumane. As Williams states his central value: "When you ignore other people completely, that is hell." [5]

Unfortunately, this personal comment comes indirectly from the playwright's poetry rather than from the characters or situations on the stage. His characters are allowed to comment more, or are more articulate, than characters of other modern playwrights, but they still have no objective and enlightened understanding of the meaning of life. They too are pessimistic figures, and their deterministic downfalls do not achieve that height of contrast with what *might have been* to produce tragedy. Seeing the world's corruption, Williams' rather fearful and pessimistic reaction is to show, not what might have been, but what is happening to the weak and unusual people for whom he is able to have a feeling. With these people, Williams was able to create great drama. But their stories are not the situation for tragedy: the tragic loser must have the potential which pessimism is unable to grant him and he must have been, at some time, a supreme winner.

III

Turning to a more specific analysis of his work, *A Streetcar Named Desire* is a pessimistic play because it is the culmination of a view of life in which evil, or at least undiminished insensitivity, conquers throughout no matter what the protagonistic forces do. Appropriate to pessimism, the play starts very late in the heroine's career; Blanche

[5] "The Angel of the Odd," p. 53.

DuBois' downfall has long since begun. We meet her at the moment she is starved for friendship, protection, and sympathy and therefore —to Williams' mind—most worth watching. In his compassion for Blanche, this very feature of loneliness is what he wants to show, and it is what he has to offer: the dramatization of the loss of love and mutual human assistance. Blanche must adjust to the new situation of Stella's lusty environment at a time when her nerves teeter on the brink of psychosis. Her psychological difficulties date back to the suicide of her boy-husband and, while it may be that this trauma was sufficient to bring Blanche to her eventual promiscuity, its importance in her character limits her tragic stature. This, a main ingredient of her pseudo-tragic flaw, is not also her greatness.

Inevitably, there is immediate conflict between Blanche's fragility and Stanley's bestiality. The moth must tempt disaster from the flame. Blanche confuses and upsets Stanley without his understanding why, and because he cannot understand why. He is bothered by her affectation, which is her protection, because he feels she is thus pretending to be superior to him. Blanche's sensitivity-value seems to flower for a moment in the Blanche–Mitch subplot but as Mitch draws closer to Blanche, Stanley reveals his information and Mitch turns away from Blanche in disgust. Momentarily dropping her pose, Blanche tries to be completely truthful about her past, but such dignity only speeds her doom. Marrying Mitch is the only way out for her, and the moment of escape passes. Finally, Blanche's superior sensibility proves to be too impregnable for moderate assaults, and Stanley's virility is challenged. While Stella is in the hospital bearing Stanley's child, ensuring the continuance of his bestial strain, Stanley rapes Blanche. Thus Williams can have society, represented by Stella, make its inevitable choice: it turns away from truth (sensitivity) and has to embrace evil (insensitivity). Stella has to commit Blanche to the state hospital rather than believe that Stanley attacked her.

The playwright's fleeting provision of an avenue of escape helps to keep the pessimism from being static, for there is some suspense in action. When Stanley stops Blanche from coming closer to security and protection with Mitch (even though Mitch's blindness to Blanche's past could hardly last long anyway), there is a clear, even Aristotelian, "discovery" and some reversal of fortune—except that Blanche's fortunes before that time were hardly very high. Stanley's machinations motivate a definite turning point in *A Streetcar Named Desire,* and his presence as antagonist aids the activity—not the rhetoric, as the case would be in *Winterset, Death of a Salesman,* or nearly any O'Neill tragedy—and theatricality of the play, even if the conclusion is still pessimistic. His weakness as a *tragic* antagonist is that he does not know why he is evil in his lack of sensitivity.

Not that Blanche is not considerably self-destroyed. She is certainly to blame for some of her moral and psychological decay. But Williams, as already seen, does not believe in original sin and conscious guilt. This produces the same limitation as a tragedy of irresponsibility, for the characters' inability to be conscious of good and bad (for all their acting out of immoral or unethical deeds) robs them of tragic significance, in that they posit no ethical–moral judgments on their decisions and behavior. Society can be too easily blamed for allowing Belle Reve as a plantation and a symbol to fall to ruin. The question is whether this loss means much or not.

Blanche is deluded and psychotic well before she gets to New Orleans and Stanley. But the specific and final means of destruction is not, as far as we know, present in her. She could go on a long while, as does the "lady of Larkspur Lotion," in Williams' play of that name. That heroine lies to herself, and she is debauched, but she has adjusted to her life with a successful delusion, pitiful as it is. As long as Blanche can keep moving, she can survive in her delusions. But Stanley, once in the picture, is her inescapable torturer and executioner.

Examining the generic faults produced by Williams' outlook, the first is in the tragic perspective. Blanche is given psychological motivations for her weakness and her sensitivity, but that sensitivity, which ought to be her greatness, is largely a function of her derangement. Sickness tends to equal sensitivity, and vice versa. The allegorical nature of the supporting characters is another weakness. Williams feels so much for Blanche, and she is so much his personal representative to the "normal" world, that he makes her enemies too easily and automatically wrong. The world that is against Blanche, or even simply unlike her, seems to contain a collective allegory of crass mankind. Thus the sensitive and the insensitive are divided too insistently and simplistically.

If, as is made so obvious to us, Stanley's stock will increase by natural selection and the apes will truly inherit the earth, there might be a tiny chance of delaying the end—as in Williams' approval of more of us being friends and lending the helping hand such as the Doctor's offered at the close of *A Streetcar Named Desire*. But obviously the process of evolution depicted is only increasing the numbers of the enemy; soon there will be none left who know and uphold the old traditions.

If there is tragedy in the play, it is actually out here in the world, not on the stage. Blanche's story, by implication only, is a tear shed for modern, anti-social man. It is tragic if we are willing to recognize an artistic, rather than a real, tragedy in man's becoming so anti-social that he communicates only in animal terms. And this is not entirely

possible in terms of what *A Streetcar Named Desire* dramatizes because the tragic meaning of the symbols of Williams' threnody for
sensitivity is not so demonstrably universal. Also, symbols, like the
statistics of war dead, cannot have as much irrevocably tragic meaning as the loss of a single great figure, whom we know directly and
fully through his accomplishments and strivings, and whose destruction shocks the society within the play into some enlightenment.

Although Williams succeeds brilliantly in making theatre, his own
words reflect the pessimism and sense of personal harm which make
his art less than tragic—by denying him some serenity and inner har-
mony as he stands back to take the larger view of his work:

> All my life I have been haunted by the obsession that to desire a thing
> or to love a thing intensely is to place yourself in a vulnerable position,
> to be a possible, if not a probable, loser of what you most want. . . .
> Having always to contend with this adversary of fear, which was some-
> times terror, gave me a certain tendency toward an atmosphere of
> hysteria and violence in my writing, an atmosphere that has existed
> in it since the beginning.[6]

Williams' increasing dread, now far greater than in the days of *A
Streetcar Named Desire,* cannot acknowledge life as going usefully
on if only for some small pinpoint of human advance—the premise
on which tragedy, as a praise of dangerous but necessary striving, is
based. He has always been too defensively close to his theme of sensi-
tivity-horribly-outnumbered to develop it as a subject for tragedy.

[6] Quoted in Goodman, *Drama on Stage,* p. 277.

The Innocence of Tennessee Williams

by Marion Magid

A European whose knowledge of America was gained entirely from the collected works of Tennessee Williams might garner a composite image of the U.S.: it is a tropical country whose vegetation is largely man-eating; it has an excessive annual rainfall and frequent storms which coincide with its mating periods; it has not yet been converted to Christianity, but continues to observe the myth of the annual death and resurrection of the sun-god, for which purpose it keeps on hand a constant supply of young men to sacrifice. Its young men are for the most part beautiful and fawnlike; an occasional rough customer turns up, but in the end he, too, is revealed as beautiful and fawnlike. Its women are alternately in a state of heat or jitters; otherwise they are Mediterranean. The country does not observe the traditional Western sexual orientation which involves the pursuit of the female by the male; instead, its young men reluctantly allow themselves to be had on those occasions when there is no way of avoiding it and when the act is signaled and underscored by portents of Elizabethan proportions. They are right in general to be of two minds regarding the sexual embrace, for it is as often as not followed by the direst consequences: cannibalism, castration, burning alive, madness, surgery in various forms ranging from lobotomy to hysterectomy, depending on the nature of the offending organ.

Perhaps the European would not be very far wrong. A culture does not consistently pay the price of admission to witness a fable which does not ensnare some part of the truth about it. Perhaps that feverish tropical set by Jo Mielziner is the land of heart's desire for Americans, as Italy has been the land of heart's desire for Englishmen, huddled all winter long around their shilling meters and damp fireplaces. In any case, watching the ladies in flowered hats queuing up for a matinee of *Sweet Bird of Youth* inevitably raises questions: How much do they understand? How much do they suspect? What do all these goings-on

"The Innocence of Tennessee Williams" by Marion Magid. From Commentary, *35 (January 1963): 34–43. Reprinted from* Commentary, *by permission. Copyright © 1963 by the American Jewish Committee.*

mean to them? Do they flock to a new play by Tennessee Williams because it is sensational, because it is "poetic," because it is both at the same time and the one quality redeems the other? Finally, do they find anything of their own experience—of love, marriage, desire, loneliness—reflected in that peculiar mirror which Williams holds up to nature?

Probably they do. Tennessee Williams is not our best, but our only American playwright since O'Neill. His imagination, magnetized though it is by the outlandish and the outré, is a kind of fever chart of our national ailments. There is, for instance, an image which runs obsessively through Williams' plays—the beautiful young man at bay, the quarry ringed by his pursuers. The mind, the sensibilities, the stomach, all recoil from this image when it is served up with obvious relish in a darkened theater, snakily choreographed by Kazan or distended on wide screen in all the glory of MGM technicolor. Yet that image is frighteningly akin to the one emblazoned not so long ago on all the front pages of the land: Meredith ringed by the Mississippi National Guard on the campus at Ole Miss; and in the background, blurred figures with clenched fists. Who knows what goes on behind those flat faces with steel-rimmed eyeglasses and slits for mouths? One has a sense that Williams dwells closer to that knowledge than other dramatists writing about us, for us, today. Though Williams has not, so far as I know, delivered himself of a single pronouncement on the question of integration, though his signature is never to be found on a petition or a full-page ad in the New York *Times,* he seems to have located the trouble spots more precisely than Arthur Miller, for instance, who deals so conscientiously with "social" questions. Williams is American in his passion for absolutes, in his longing for purity, in his absence of ideas, in the extreme discomfort with which he inhabits his own body and soul, in his apocalyptic vision of sex, which like all apocalyptic visions sacrifices mere accuracy for the sake of intensity. Intensity is the crucial quality of Williams' art, and he is perhaps most an American artist in his reliance upon and mastery of surface techniques for achieving this effect.

One result is that Williams' plays cannot be talked about except in their performance. Ever since 1947, when *A Streetcar Named Desire* was produced under the direction of Elia Kazan and starring Marlon Brando, Jessica Tandy, and Kim Hunter, with a stage setting by Jo Mielziner, the pattern for rendition of a Williams play has remained as fixed as a Kabuki dance. Other hands than Kazan's have since dimmed the lights, set the underbrush to quivering and on occasion gilded the lily, yet the results have always been, when successful—that is, when "like a play by Tennessee Williams"—approximations of that *ur*-Williams production.

There is first of all the matter of lighting. As Eric Bentley observed, Kazan sees the world, especially Williams' world, as phantasmagoria. "Don't turn the lights on," Blanche gasps in *Streetcar* and Kazan passed the word on to the electricians. Nor have they been turned on since. Doing so would dispel the shadows, the evanescence, the sense of undefined shapes and meanings lurking in the foliage. In Hollywood, the word "air" is used to designate atmosphere, the intangible stuff of which dreams are made. Directors in the throes of creation have been known to cry out for "more air"—which means the opposite of what it seems to mean: not clarity nor breathing space nor the light of day, but the baying of bloodhounds, the waving of palm fronds, the lonely clarinet solo, the voices of offstage potion peddlers raised in song. The milieu of Williams' plays lends itself especially well to this hot (Southern) "air" treatment. One suspects that, after *Streetcar*, Williams worked with an image in his mind's eye closer to the South of Broadway than to the actual South.

The second element is timing. Kazan is the virtuoso of a certain kind of tension on stage. His method might be called the technique of unexpected syncopation. The regular to-and-fro buildup of a climactic scene, particularly of an encounter between two actors, is slightly distorted. Pauses are a trifle longer than expected, or a trifle shorter. Long speeches are broken up in eccentric ways, so that unexpected words ring out in the electric silence. No Williams play is complete without the participation of at least one, preferably more, actors who have been trained at the Actors' Studio or temples of the same persuasion, where they have perfected their versions of this curious syncopation. This mode of diction has by now become a convention of contemporary American theater in the past two decades. Its components are mainly twofold: since it was originally developed by the Group Theater in its attempt to render "realistically" the rhythms of urban, and especially New York, life, it has more than a trace in it of Yiddish inflection as well as Yiddish phrasing; at the same time it has been updated by hipster gesture and talk. The diction can now be heard nightly on those serious hour-long television dramas which frequently give the impression of being dubbed, so many preparatory lip movements does the actor go through before he works around to the crisis of utterance. This nervous medley acts as an assurance to the spectator that harrowing as the content is of what is spoken, what is unspoken is even worse. What is said is the less important half; the better half is the silence.

Williams writes the ideal "line" for this mode of delivery. It is a long line, which achieves its most striking effects through a Steinian repetitiveness, through the use of unexpected archaisms, and the insertion of unexpected "literary" words and ironically elegant turns of phrase. It is a stylized rendering of Southern diction, which is more self-conscious, more evasive, but also more imaginative than Northern speech. The odd thing is that nearly all of Williams' characters speak this language, regardless of class or place of origin, and it is to be heard even in the grunts of Stanley and Mitch in their more pensive moments.

When a Williams libretto is placed in the hands of an actor whose rendition is tailored to it, the result is an orgy of syncopation just this side of hysteria. It has been remarked that Williams writes great parts for actresses, but only for a certain kind of actress. She must bring to the part a fund of that particular kind of nervous intensity that we associate with Geraldine Page, Maureen Stapleton, or Lois Smith. The champion performance of all time in The Syncopated Mode was the one given by Geraldine Page in *Summer and Smoke* in 1951. It was this performance which brought her stardom and spawned legions of imitations that are still among us—actresses who express emotion by plucking at their forearms and the ever-present brooch at their throats, who issue declarations with an upward inflection and ask questions with a downward one.

The actress who lacks this particular intensity is as fatally out of place as a prima donna singing in English with an Italian opera company. A case in point was that of Shelley Winters, who played the female predator in *The Night of the Iguana*. Miss Winters is not on the brink of hysteria, she does not even seem neurotic, much less bizarre. Dressed in blue jeans and a hastily buttoned man's shirt, she romped through the part of the bitch hotelkeeper looking like nothing so much as a plump athletics counselor at a girl's camp. Common sense as well as the sense of humor rebelled against the idea that she represented that ogre-female, the hideous embodiment of the life force, which is central to Williams' vision of life. Lacking its center, the play slowly fell apart.

All of which are some of the reasons why a successful Williams play in full regalia does not seem written and produced so much as masterminded; it is more like the perfect crime than an artistic undertaking. Williams' vision is not only fulfilled, it is over-fulfilled by Kazan's technique, which is to keep the play in a state of constant explosive motion. Perhaps this is one reason why it does not linger in the mind. Its effect is all in the seeing and quivering at the moment of seeing, a series of shocks to the eye and to the nervous system which renders the viewer captive. Occasionally one has an impulse to shout "Stop!" when some particularly questionable assertion has been made onstage, but it has already flitted away, been swallowed up in the chiaroscuro. It is this shimmering motion that most of the critics praise when they invoke Williams' good qualities—his "elusiveness," his "poeticism." It is as though on Broadway that larger ambiguity which is a characteristic of great art can be achieved merely by a blurring of outline. Dim the lights, provide a clarinet solo or the tinkling of a jukebox, buttress the action with a gathering storm and if possible add a symbol or two which seems to flicker on and off like a neon light, saying: "I may look like an iguana, but what I really am is a symbol." Then all efforts to discern what the playwright is actually saying will be dismissed as pedantry, offensive to the "magical" nature of the theatrical occasion.

Lately, however, Williams has been getting a bad press, though for the wrong reasons. Certain of his motifs have become so insistent and so unmistakable that they no longer quite scurry away unnoticed into the underbrush. Yet Williams' vision has not really changed so much between *Streetcar,* which was hailed as our only American tragedy, and *Sweet Bird of Youth,* which outraged even Kenneth Tynan. It seems unjust of the critics to have taken Williams to their bosoms when he hinted coyly at the unspeakable and to chide him when he speaks a bit more clearly about it.

The total effect of Williams' work has been to plunge ordinary conceptions of the male-female relation into such disorder that the services of a Harry Stack Sullivan seem needed to straighten them out again. The first of these grand subversions was the figure of Stanley Kowalski, which appeared before the American public and before the world in the person of Marlon Brando. Though numerous actors have since played the part, Brando remains forever etched in memory as the embodiment of American malehood, and Kowalski is probably the most famous male figure in modern drama. Doubtless at this moment Brando's Korean counterpart is playing the role in whatever passes at the Seoul Repertory Company for a torn t-shirt.

Kazan, who likes to get down to brass tacks, described Kowalski in his celebrated notes to the production of *Streetcar* as "a walking penis." Whatever that would look like (the imagination is certainly compelled), Brando's rendition of it came out as something more ambivalent. His mincing interpretation of the role may even have struck sophisticated members of the audience as a brilliant example of post-Freudian insight: the walking phallus must necessarily take on some suspicious mannerisms: we all know about overcompensation, and what is brutality but the fear of cowardice and impotence?

Leaving Brando's performance out of it and taking Kowalski at face value, as written by Williams—what are we to make of him? Even forgetting temporarily certain cultural data—that members of the lower middle class are rather more inclined toward the sham genteel in their sexual mores than toward the nobly savage, and that it is primarily college graduates who are as conscientious about their sex

life as though it were some humanist obligation—one still wonders
how Stella and Stanley ever got together. How did Stella ever get
over those initial hurdles—Stanley's table manners, Stanley's prefer-
ences in dress, Stanley's recreational interests, Stanley's friends, Stanley's stupidity? If we accept Stanley as ape, the character of Stella
ceases to be interesting except clinically. Williams claims allegiance
with Lawrence in his philosophy of sex, yet in the creation of Kowalski he forgets utterly Lawrence's basic lesson—that profound sexual experience civilizes, humanizes, lends grace and delicacy. Lady
Chatterley is attracted specifically by the natural aristocracy of the
gamekeeper which his skill and power as a lover only confirm. Despite
his presence on the stage in satin pajamas and his continued invoca-
tion of the "colored lights" we do not really believe in the instinctive
animal beauty (purity?) of Stanley in bed because out of it he behaves
with such benighted crudity. Did Stanley rape Stella, too, just by way
of a how-do-you-do? Do all women burn to be raped? Is this the
locker-room fantasy that is Williams' version of animal purity?

"They come together with low, animal moans," the stage directions
say. Earlier Stella launches into the first of those hushed sexual confidences which run through all of Williams' plays and ring such an
astonishingly false note. "I can hardly stand it when he's away for a
night," says Stella. "When he's away for a week I nearly go wild. . . .
And when he comes back I cry on his lap like a baby. . . ." It is
hard to know what is more unpleasant in this image: the overt sentimentality it expresses, or the latent brutality it masks: a fascination
with the image of the helpless creature under the physical domination
of another, accepting his favors with tears of gratitude. That the emotion of gratitude is not the predominant one that women feel for
their lovers seems to have escaped Williams, fixated as he seems to
be upon the delights his heroes must be capable of affording. Later
Stella's breathless sexual confidences will be echoed by Serafina delle
Rose, describing her husband's prodigious feats in bed, and by Margaret describing the absolute "indifference" of Brick, which makes
him the perfect lover. When there is no woman on the scene to give
testimony, the heroes themselves oblige with weary chronicles of the
services they have rendered scores of women: Val in *Orpheus Descending*, refusing to serve any longer as "stud" to women like the impatient
Carol; Chance Wayne in *Sweet Bird of Youth* describing the legions
of lonely women whom he has taught about love; Shannon in *Night
of the Iguana* confiding his rape at the hands of an adolescent girl.
At the center of most of Williams' plays there is the same slightly re-
pellent pas de deux: the man austere, eager to keep his purity; the
woman turning to him like Potiphar's wife unto Joseph.

The foregoing belongs, in Williams' world, to the category of "corruption." When he describes "pure" love, one expects hoots from the gallery—but perhaps again the gallery is hungering for any version of that fabled sentiment that Williams can manage to offer. "Pure" love in Williams—which antedates the hero's initiation into "corruption" (spoken darkly, with a faint slurring)—generally takes place in aquatic environs when both the hero and the heroine were very young. The heroine—Val's chance encounter on a houseboat off the Florida coast, Chance Wayne's true love by the Gulf Stream—is generally an exceedingly pale girl with long blond hair—ethereal to the point of incorporeality. In *Sweet Bird,* dramatizing one of those fervid paradoxes that Williams so loves, Heavenly, the "corrupted" pure love, rides at the head of a political caravan, dressed "all in whaat . . . laak a virgin . . ." though she's had that—operation—(spoken darkly and crooningly) "done" on her. . . . How strange to find Williams, the disciple of Lawrence, talking about physical (corrupt) and spiritual (pure) love.

A Streetcar Named Desire—
Nietzsche Descending

by Joseph N. Riddell

To see *A Streetcar Named Desire* as a realistic slice-of-life is to mistake its ambitious theme; to find its social protest is to misread the surface, for just as in *The Glass Menagerie*, Williams gets in his social licks while groping for a more universal statement. It is not, however, in its subthemes that *Streetcar* fails but in its overabundant intellectualism, its aspiration to say something about man and his civilization, its eclectic use and often contradictory exploitation of ideas. Williams has been called neo-Lawrencean, placing him in that assemblage of revived romantics and primitives in revolt against a sodden, effeminate age, but he is a Nietzschean as well, if in a very imperfect and perhaps over-impetuous way.

In *Streetcar*, as in several other plays, Williams borrows from Nietzsche in great chunks, often undigested, using his sources with that liberal freedom that has become characteristic of the American artist in search of a theme. Readers of *Streetcar* are soon aware of the problems this creates, for they are faced at the beginning by a welter of symbols—both linguistic and theatrical—that force upon the realistic surface a conscious, almost allegorical pattern. Williams has, at various times, had less success with the integration of his excessive symbolism and his theme, as in the satyr-like spiritualism of *The Rose Tattoo* or the panic-homosexual-psychoanalytic motif of *Suddenly Last Summer*. But even in *Streetcar* one must begin with a contradiction between his intellectual design and the militant primitivism of the theme; or to use a philosophical gloss, one must begin with Nietzsche's Apollonian–Dionysian conflict, in an almost literal sense.

Williams has offered what he considers a serious rationale for his kind of drama in "The Timeless World of a Play," with which he prefaced an edition of *The Rose Tattoo*. The argument is dubious but

"A Streetcar Named Desire—*Nietzsche Descending*" by *Joseph N. Riddell. From* Modern Drama, *5 (February 1963): 421–30. Reprinted by permission of* Modern Drama.

revealing. As if he had misinterpreted Eliot's remark, that art expresses a primitive truth which uses the phenomena of civilization because that is all it has to use, Williams makes a plea for the drama as a non-temporal stage whose characters are removed from and purified of their distracting social contexts. The play, he insists, arrests time, snatching the "eternal out of the desperately fleeting," penetrating beyond the social façade to the innate man beneath. Anyone familiar with the devices of *The Glass Menagerie* will recognize that he is to take a cue from the opening and closing sequences and filter out the tawdriness of the middle, the mundane stuff that blights the purity of the characters' hearts and actions. Life, it implies, is maligned by the conditions of living. There is more than social protest here, and there is certainly no area for the tragic.

This strangely persistent romantic notion that the idea of man is some pre-rational, mystical, universal oneness which civilization with its artificial forms travesties is indifferent to the artist's strategic assumption that between man and his conditions there is indeed a plausible and symbolic connection. What Kenneth Burke has termed the strategy of scene–act ratio is certainly fundamental to a fully realized stage, from the mythic to the realistic—as Francis Fergusson's important study, *The Idea of a Theater,* proves. (One can make this observation, I think, without being callous about social inequity or injustice, without saying that each man deserves his environment.) Williams himself depends extensively on the symbolic ratio of character to scene, yet he seems to ask for two contradictory things: that we endure his realistic surface—and indeed be entertained and informed by it—and that we respond more truly by extirpating the temporal and spiritually involving ourselves in the purified world beneath. In effect, the symbolic scene should add meaningful dimensions to the play, yet not be a temporal setting at all. Furthermore, he is insisting that in the drama individuation of character is only a convenience and that character finally resolves into the archetypes of a morality play—or better, a pre-morality dance of life. This is something else again than saying that a character must be universal: it claims that he is pure essence. In sum, it is a rather narrow variation on the prevailing critical thesis of drama as ritual, only Williams, instead of making the valid observation that characters constitute parts of a whole in the play, steps outside drama to postulate a spiritual, primordial idea of man which the play evokes.

In *The Birth of Tragedy,* Nietzsche describes the difference between the chorus and the virgins bearing laurel branches, in his characteristic Greek play, as a symbolic antithesis of the Dionysian and the Apollonian: the one characterized by a oneness of passion and metaphysical character, the other by restraint, order, and by individuation of charac-

ter. His metaphysical tension between the Dionysian and the Apollonian natures is, in the simplest terms, his definition of tragedy; but as
Walter Kaufmann has convincingly shown, to accentuate the Dionysian at the expense of its antithesis, as is popularly done, is to misread
Nietzsche's famous metaphor. Indeed, says Kaufmann, Nietzsche is the
Apollonian at heart, who has come to recognize the effeteness of civilization that exhausts or extirpates its vital creative energies (its Dionysian self) in empty forms, that sacrifices vitality for order. The Dionysian spirit, then, he finds necessary but potentially chaotic, unless
channelled and put to creative use by the Apollonian. In Greek drama
at its height Nietzsche discovered just the proper tension—so necessary
to his conception of man's tragic dignity—before the intrusion of
Socratic reason, admirable as it was, led to a forced exclusion of the
Dionysian vitality, and subsequently, in secular epigenism and Christianity, to an ethical world view that sought to suppress all disordered
passions. The point of all this is that Nietzsche, the supposed progeni-
tor of post-ethical romanticism, is an antagonist of romanticism, which
he repudiated in a later preface to *The Birth of Tragedy* as a kind of
unrestrained, chaotic investment in emotion for emotion's sake. In his
later work, Kaufmann shows, Nietzsche reconstructed Dionysus in the
character of an ideal divinity (a combination of Dionysus–Apollo), so
that the repudiated Dionysus and the one with whom Nietzsche at last
identified himself are two different gods. In sum, Nietzsche's conception was dialectical, Dionysus needing Apollo like the id an ego, or
vitality form; and ultimately the two blend in an ideal of tragic beauty.
It is the influence of Jung, with his radically romantic world of archetypes, that has done so much to motivate our artists' return to the
primitive, but the misplaced emphasis on Nietzsche's Dionysus is no
less important.

Willfully or not, Williams seems to commit the error of popular
misinterpretation, not in the sense that he writes a drama to the
Nietzschean tune but that he exploits Nietzsche's metaphor to elucidate
and justify his own vaguely formed vision of man. At times his play
gains intensity of realization from his obsession with the conflict between creative impulse and civilized decorum; on other occasions it
suffers from a divisiveness caused by its lack of tension, its undialectical
character, its deliberately one-sided argument. This very lack of tension—thematic not dramatic—precludes tragedy and leaves us in a
very startling way with a thesis play of sorts and a series of violent if
symbolic actions.

The setting of *Streetcar* is a combination of raw realism and deliberate fantasy, a world very much of our society yet timeless and innocent,
without ethical dimensions. Williams' evocation of a mythical Elysia
suggests a world of the guiltless, of spring and sunlight (though his is

shaded, a night world), a pre-Christian paradise where life and passion are one and good. The "Elysian Fields" is New Orleans in several senses: the Elysia where life is pursued on a primitive level beyond or before good and evil. This, I think, must be insisted upon, for the play is a deliberate outrage against conventional morality, a kind of immoralist's protest in the manner if not the style of Gide. The impressionistic scene, lyrical and with an aura of vitality that "attenuates the atmosphere of decay," is a Dionysian world of oneness, where there is an "easy mingling of races" and the pagan chromatics of a "blue piano" provide rhythms for a Bacchic revel.

One does not have to force his interpretation. The humorous vulgarity of the opening section is self-consciously symbolic, abrupt on the level of realism but carefully designed to signify the play's two worlds. Stanley's appearance in his masculine vigor, carrying a "red stained package from the butcher's," competes with the mythical aura of the scene. The implied virility of his gesture in tossing the package to Stella, her suggestive response, and the carefree vigor of their unconcern with time defines succinctly a kind of world that is immediate yet infused with an intensity beyond the real. The scene then pans down on Blanche in her demure and fragile dress, garishly overrefined, overwhelmed by life, out of place in Elysium. She has arrived, we learn, by way of a Freudian streetcar named "Desire," transferring to one called "Cemeteries." The psychoanalytic devices are obvious: Stanley's gesture is vital—prurient yet pure; Blanche on her figurative streetcars has been a pawn of the phallus of desire. If she is a cliché of southern literature, she is likewise the incarnate deathwish of civilization. Williams takes his epigraph from Hart Crane's "The Broken Tower," and perhaps also his streetcar from Crane's "For the Marriage of Faustus and Helen," though the poet's work soon jumps its Freudian tracks to become his Faustian artist's symbolic conveyance to a Helen-ideal. Like Crane Williams finds love in man's "broken world" a "visionary company," an "instant in the wind" suffused with time's desperation. Blanche and Stanley become antiphonal figures in a choric exchange of ideas. The Freudian–Nietzschean paraphernalia operate in close conjunction as a massive assault on the futility of our civilized illusions, which Williams always portrays as both necessary and self-destructive.

The Apollonian–Dionysian motif is vigorously accentuated, but not exactly to Nietzsche's purpose. Blanche, as her name implies, is the pallid, lifeless product of her illusions, of a way of life that has forfeited its vigor through what she later calls her family's "epic fornications," perversions of a healthy procreative sex. Her "Belle Reve," the family plantation, rests in Apollo's orchard, "Laurel," Mississippi. She is in every sense the sum of an exhausted tradition that is the

essence of sophistication and culture run down into the appearance
that struggles to conceal rapacity. Her life is a living division of two
warring principles, desire and decorum, and she is the victim of civilization's attempt to reconcile the two in a morality. Her indulgent
past is a mixture of sin and romance, reality and illusion, the excesses
of the self and the restraints of society. Williams has followed Nietzsche in translating what is essentially metaphysical hypothesis into
a metaphor of psychological conflict. Her schizoid personality is a
drama of man's irreconcilable split between animal reality and moral
appearance, or as Freud put it figuratively, a mortal conflict of id
against ego and superego. Blanche lives in a world of shades, of
Chinese lanterns, of romantic melodies that conjure up dream worlds,
of perversions turned into illusory romances, of alcoholic escape, of
time past—the romantic continuity of generations to which she looks
for identity—and of Christian morality that refines away, or judicially
and morally vitiates, animal impulse. Thus, she is driven by guilt
over the very indulgences that give Stanley's life a vital intensity.

    As her anti-self, Stanley is as consciously created. Born under the
sign of Capricorn, the Goat—as Blanche was born under the sign of
Virgo—he is, according to the stage directions, a veritable Pan–Dionysus, the "gaudy seed-bearer," the embodiment of "animal joy" whose
life "has been pleasure with women, the giving and taking of it, not
with weak indulgence, dependently, but with the power and pride of
a richly feathered male bird among hens." He is identified variously
with the goat, the cat, and the locomotive, three rather obvious symbols that define his sex-centered life and repeatedly disturb Blanche's
tenuous psychic balance. It is revealing, too, that Blanche very early
sees in Stanley a source to reinvigorate the DuBois blood. This is no
genetic plan but, on Blanche's part, a pathetic hope for the revival of
the old dissipated values. She finds her evil lying in the blood and her
values in the illusions which can explain away moral indiscretions.
Those who acclaimed Williams' earthly Inferno mistook the symbolic
scene for realism, failing to note the inverted image of a pagan Para-
diso, where civilized values are in desuetude and the blood dictates a
pulsating order of intensity and calm. The characters are to be judged,
if at all, in degree to their response to the rhythm.

    The love of Stanley for Stella describes precisely this rhythm of
violence and reconciliation, and it exists beyond Blanche's ken. The
jazz motif which alternates with the polka music—in contrast to
Blanche's affinity for the romantic waltz—establishes the primitive
norm to which each character adapts or suffers a dissonant psychic
shock. All the old devices are here. The animal appetite is equated
with the spiritual appetite for wholeness, and must be satisfied on its
own terms, not those of a pre-established ethic. Stanley and Stella

move freely between elemental sex and mystical experience, and Williams lends to their relationship every possible symbolic device to enforce the mystical oneness of their union. On the other hand, Blanche's neurotic reveries emerge from the internal drama of conflicting passions caused by her moral conscience. They are to be described, I suppose, in the familiar psychological terms of repression and transference, though the drama seems to lay the cause not the cure, at the foot of consciousness and reason. Blanche's obsessive bathing is a nominal gesture of guilt and wished-for redemption, which becomes one of the play's recurrent symbols, along with the piano, locomotives, cats, telephones, and drink.

Alcohol plays a dual role. If it is one source of Blanche's hysterical escape from moral contingencies, it is likewise the stimulant of the Bacchic rites that punctuate Stanley's life. Drunkenness, indeed, is the physiological analogue for Dionysian ecstasy, as the dream–illusion symbolizes the Apollonian state. Blanche drinks to induce illusion, to extirpate moral contradictions that stand between her and the pure "Belle Reve." But for Stanley, drink induces a state of conviviality and conjugal oneness that has meaning only because it is counterbalanced by violent disturbances of irrational passion. His moments of violence are caused invariably by an external intrusion into that oneness, though violence is an integral part of the blood rhythm by which he lives. The rape scene must be read in this context, even though it is popularly recorded as a combination of unremitting realism and oversuggestive theatrics.

A closer look at a sequence of the play's middle scenes will, I think, underscore the way in which Williams exploits this primitive rhythm while moving his play along in temporal sequence. Scene Three opens with some down-to-earth conversation at the poker table, set in the timeless impression of what the stage directions call a "Van Gogh" canvas. Blanche and Stella have gone out for dinner, a show, and drinks. They return soon after the scene opens, bringing into the masculine world a feminine interruption. Blanche's conduct is vulgarly suggestive, and a combination of her sexual gestures toward Mitch and her playing of the radio—first the derivative and conventionalized Latin rhythms of Xavier Cugat, then Viennese waltzes—leads conclusively to Stanley's violence upon Stella. The motivation here is not unsubtle. Stanley is incited to toss the radio out the window, and Stella responds with an uncharacteristic reproach: *"Drunk—drunk—animal thing, you!"* Stella for the moment echoes Blanche, judging her husband by the values of her old life, censuring the animal vitality that has rescued her from Blanche's effete world. The dramatic rhythm that completes the scene was the perfect opportunity for Brando's "method." Stanley's impulsive beating of Stella, her withdrawal, the moments of waiting while Stanley bellows goat-like in the wings, and the animal sensuality of their reconciliation fulfills the pattern of sexual will that concludes in a transcendental ecstasy of love. At the end Stella is once more within her husband's primitive embrace, to which she brings the spiritual, even cosmic, balance that his unformed vigor demands. But Blanche sees the whole affair only as "violence," upon her decorous sensibility and "Belle Reve." The real violence is the forced recognition of the conflicting drives within herself.

Scene Four opens with the dramatic contrast between Stella and Blanche, the one "narcotized" like the face of an "Eastern idol," by her union of the previous night, the other pressed to the edge of anxiety. The entire scene is a drama of misunderstanding, accentuated by Blanche's wild but purposeless effort to rescue her sister, and thus the family, from animalistic forces. At one point she is driven to protest against Stella's mystical indifference to the night's affair by asking if her sister had cultivated a "Chinese philosophy," and one is not to miss the suggestion of identity between the Oriental calm and the sexual holiness of the two lovers. The scene moves through a series of neurotically aimless gestures on Blanche's part to a frenetic conclusion in her diatribe against an animalistic world. Immediately before the outburst, the cleavage between the two worlds is underlined:

> *Stella.* But there are things that happen between a man and a woman in the dark—that sort of make everything else seem—unimportant. (*Pause*)
> *Blanche.* What you are talking about is brutal desire—just—Desire!— the name of that rattle-trap streetcar that bangs through the Quarter, up one old narrow street and down another . . .
> *Stella.* Haven't you ever ridden on that streetcar?
> *Blanche.* It brought me here.—Where I'm not wanted and where I'm ashamed to be . . .

Love is the mystical leaven that for Stella—who, one presumes, is the ideal polarity of Stanley's realistic self—elevates the animal to the spiritual and makes them one. Uncomprehendingly, Blanche bursts out "plainly" against man's "anthropological" heritage, concluding her argument, that Stella must join the legions of culture, with a revealing plea: "Don't—don't hang back with the brutes!" There is implicit in Blanche's remarks—made against the background of the inevitable train whistle, while Stanley stands in the wings—the call of history and progress, and the Apollonian illusion of reconciliation through culture, the arts, beauty. Against this rhetoric Williams juxtaposes the action of Stanley as a reminder of the necessary vitality in any creative dream, the incipient animal within the human. The conclusion of the scene once again resolves into the passionate order of sexual transcendence, leaving Blanche pathetically and helplessly within the hollow ring of her argument.

Scene Five offers much of the same, with Blanche's quest for escape from reality played off against the fight between Steve and Eunice, which ends in a reconciliation of "goat-like screeches" while Blanche makes seductive gestures toward a bewildered newsboy under the illusion of medieval romance. And Scene Six, after an interlude of Blanche's forced prudery to stave off Mitch and her own irrepressible desires, ends in a violent confession of her horror at the suicide of her homosexual husband. Confession here acts to release her momentarily into the ecstasy of union with Mitch, which in turn leads only in the subsequent scene to guilt, ritualistic bathing, and the intense clash of Stanley's brute truths about her past and Blanche's "make-believe" rationalizations. The structure of these scenes is sound and predictable, if not sensational. There is no act division in the play, perhaps because the theme disallows a syllogistic progression of human actions in time, while demanding a recurring pattern of conflict and reconcilia- tion that accords with the natural rhythms of passion. Realistically viewed, Stanley's world is a dreadfully boring repetition of acts, but symbolically, it fulfills a timeless, ritualistic cycle. In a sense, the progressive action required by the play's realism is at odds with the archetypal inner action, which is no better revealed than in the con- tradictory function of the climax.

The rape that concludes Scene Ten serves a double structural pur- pose of resolving that scene in a moment of passion and bringing the play to its climax. There is some confusion, however, between the rape as a plausible realistic act and as a symbolic ravishing of the Apollonian by the Dionysian self. For if the play's symbolic conflict is to be resolved, as is suggested by Stanley's cryptic statement to Blanche that "We've had this date with each other from the begin- ning," the final scene is not so clear in its implications. Blanche, in her psychologically ingrown virginity, is driven further into herself and her dream, not released, and is handed over to Williams' modern priest, the psychoanalyst, for care. There is an unclear mingling of themes here. Blanche at first withdraws from the doctor and matron— stereotyped, masculinized symbols of the state institution—only to capitulate to the doctor when he personalizes himself by removing his professional appearance. It is, then, suggested that Blanche is to be returned to the world, the one outside Stanley's and Stella's Elysium of mystical "love," where the necessity of illusion plays its ambiguous role. Stanley's act becomes in this context an egregious breach of morality—yet the play's conclusion obscures moral judgment.

Blanche, of course, comes to symbolize a civilized world that cannot face its essential and necessary primitive self, and thus exists in a

constant state of internecine anxiety. Unlike suppliants of the Dionysian cult, she cannot devour the god whose self is the wafer of regen-
eration. And Williams offers, as he does elsewhere, the psychoanalyst
as surrogate artist–priest, who must reconstruct the fragments of personality by absolving conflict and its attendant guilt. I hesitate to con-
ceive Williams' conclusion in strict psychological terms, for he tempers
psychoanalysis with a rather indeterminate mysticism. His analyst–
priest is not the Freudian doctor whose purpose is to purge the irrational and reorient the self by making suppressed conflicts conscious
and intelligible. This seems to be the human gesture of the analyst in
Suddenly Last Summer, but even there Williams conceives of him as
a kind of artist, remolding one personality out of the wasteful fragments of another. Williams indicates no clear trust in the rational
solution. Blanche's fate and the future of her world remain ambiguous,
but Stanley and Stella are reconciled by a dual motivation: Stella by
the illusion that she must unquestioningly accept things as they are
and not complicate them with moral suspicions; Stanley by an animal
need that provides spiritual fulfillment. If the Dionysian self never
senses conflict, he remains nevertheless a marginal figure, his ecstatic
world beyond our realization. We are left with Blanche's pathos, and
the ambiguous suggestions that through "love" she will be returned
not to the emptiness of "Belle Reve" but to a civilized world of more
substantial illusions. If she is the tragic victim of a world of unrestrained animal appetite, she must regain, even through compassion
and understanding, some of the vitality (and thus the primitivism) exhausted by her heirs. And Stanley's world is left, in the play's concluding words, to repeat itself timelessly in a ritual of "seven-card stud,"
which must stand as a reproach to if not a solution for the etiolated
rituals of a civilization that excludes the realities of the blood.

   The confusions of *Streetcar* must be attributed, it seems to me, to
three things: the play's insistence on an amoral scene, in which the
Dionysian rhythm is retailed as a norm; the use of psychological motifs to authenticate primitivism; and the deliberate exploitation of
intellectual themes and symbols in the cause of anti-intellectualism.
Williams' rejection of contemporary civilization takes the easy form
of repudiating the moral masks which suffocate natural man, but he
in no way envisions the human tensions that Nietzsche found so
integral to man's tragic dignity, nor does he offer in contrast a plausible
antithesis to his rejection of civilization—except a vaguely subscribed
"love." This is not to say that one should expect Williams to provide
either moral or intellectual answers. But to offer the purely Dionysian
as a primitive order beyond morality is essentially a negative commentary, even though Williams presumes to stress an innate good in

vitalism. The dialogue that constitutes tragedy is stifled, and with it Blanche's cry.

Williams fabricates his Dionysian norm without the judicious insight he employed in *The Glass Menagerie,* where the individual rises above the world's decadence by coming to moral terms with himself and the bitter realities of that world. In the purely Dionysian world, as Nietzsche pointed out and as Williams fails to grasp, individuality must be sacrificed to the universal unconscious and the tensions of dramatic conflict dissolved into chaos. Dionysianism pure is chaos and not simply the primitive order suggested in the rise and fall of blood passions. Universal innocence forfeits moral judgment, for innocence is capable of the extremes of action (including both good and evil) and thus escapes morality. Williams disallows the moralist's conclusions against Stanley's world. It is amoral (primitive and thus chaotic and partial) but made whole at least through the spiritual complement of Stella. Her role, which seems to be defined with calculated purpose early in the play, never develops functionally, and her action in the final scene fails to clarify the play. This attenuation of Stella's role is a major factor in the play's unresolved conclusion. Thus, Stanley's unpalatable world is not to be seen as rapacious but as part of the essential and inescapable reality of things. What Williams misses, in attaching now a moral judgment, now symbolic innocence to his animal functionaries is that his final scene does insinuate moral predilections while the substance of the play has obviated the moral scene for the ritualistic. Blanche's world, our world, begs for sympathy in its very throes. Williams, having attended its funeral, is loath to depart the grave, for he discovers too late that he can return only to Stanley's virile but chaotic game. The play shocks not where it is supposed to—by a deft inversion of the prevailing norms, as in Gide's *The Immoralist*—but in its realism, which it does not successfully manage to suspend. *Streetcar* is torn asunder, like Orpheus by the Maenads, by overextended symbolism and an excess of self-consciousness. The simile is not altogether unrelated to Williams' total achievement.

Most Famous of Streetcars

by W. David Sievers

Of all recent dramas, *A Streetcar Named Desire* is the quintessence of Freudian sexual psychology. Anyone familiar with Williams' one-act plays has seen clearly foreshadowed the development of Blanche DuBois of *Streetcar*. *The Lady of Larkspur Lotion* shows what a Blanche might have become if she had not met her nemesis in Stanley Kowalski—a derelict prostitute living on delusions in the French Quarter; a writer across the hall gives what might be the rationale for all the Blanches: "Is she to be blamed because it is necessary for her to compensate for the cruel deficiencies of reality by the exercise of a little—what shall I say?—God-given imagination?" Williams' *Portrait of a Madonna* is another one-act which shows an old and still virginal version of Mathilda or Blanche manufacturing illusions—fantasies of rape and pregnancy—until she is taken away by the same doctor and nurse who come for Blanche when the *Streetcar* reaches the end of its tragic line.

A Streetcar Named Desire (1947) depicts characters who are volatile, colorful, deeply real for our times. With a mastery no playwright has equalled in this century, Williams arranges in a compelling theatrical pattern the agonized sexual anxiety of a girl caught between *id* and *ego–ideal*. Blanche DuBois arrives at her sister's squalid, dilapidated home in the French Quarter of New Orleans unconsciously playing a role, that of the gracious, refined lady of the old South—the same ego–ideal which Amanda held for herself. It is a sincere role, for it is the only one a sheltered Southern belle was raised to know. Blanche finds her sister, Stella, married to the shirtless Stanley Kowalski, a superbly original character who would have delighted D. H. Lawrence. "Since earliest manhood the center of his life has been pleasure with women, the giving and taking of it, not with weak indulgence, dependently, but with the power and pride of a richly feathered male bird among hens." Stanley immediately finds himself challenged and baffled by Blanche,

"*Most Famous of Streetcars.*" *From* Freud on Broadway, *by W. David Sievers (New York: Hermitage House, Inc., 1955). Reprinted by permission of Mrs. Lucy Sievers.*

whose "airs" are a defiance to his manhood and unconsciously dare him to conquer her. Blanche is overcome by his sensuality and almost vomits. She has met her match, and the play becomes an unconscious sexual battle between the two—although the principal battlefield is within Blanche herself.

Her sister, Stella (for Star) is anything but a star. She is a healthy housewife, adjusted to reality, expecting a child, and serenely happy in her physical relationship with Stanley. With unconscious jealousy, Blanche tries to split them apart and convince Stella that Stanley is an ape, "something sub-human, thousands of years old, a stone age cave man." In spite of Stanley's explosive temper, however, their violent quarrels always end in passionate reconciliation, and for Stella it is the "things that happen between a man and a woman in the dark" that make her life in the slums of New Orleans worthwhile.

It is this relationship that keeps Blanche in sexual anxiety, which she keeps in check with hot baths and shots of whiskey. Her almost hysterical drive is to find protection and security, which in the Southern chivalric code could only come from a gallant gentleman. She believes that she has found such a man in Mitch, a friend of Stanley's. With him Blanche is all coyness and charm, shielding a naked light bulb with a little colored lantern—which Williams makes the symbolic theme of the play: people who cannot face reality try to pretty it up with the colored shades of illusion. Her efforts to play the lady with Mitch irk Stanley until he spills to Stella the scandal which he has been motivated to dig up on "Dame Blanche": she had been a prostitute in Laurel and had been thrown out of the worst hotel in town. Stanley's ironic tale of her nymphomania, complete with soldiers from the nearby army camp and the loss of her position as a schoolteacher for seducing a 17-year-old boy, is told contrapuntally against the giddy singing of Blanche in the hot bath—"It's only a paper moon . . ." In fact, Williams throughout *Streetcar* has orchestrated the sounds of the French Quarter with a superb musical feeling—its sexual throbbing, its sensual "blue piano" playing, the voices of Mexican women, the violent fights of the couple upstairs, and the hallucinatory return of the Varsouvienne music to Blanche as she recalls the tragic story of her love for her husband. Only to Mitch is she able to reveal the details of her marriage to a sweetfaced, poetic boy who turned out to be a homosexual and who shot himself after she had found him with a man. Mitch in turn confides to her of his sick mother, and betrays himself as a boy with an Oedipus complex, wanting to escape his mother yet loyally worshipping her. In their mutual loneliness, Blanche and Mitch embrace passionately, and there is in this scene promise that marriage might be a salvation for them. But the tragedy for Blanche is that she has already whetted the appetite and sadism of Stanley,

and now he becomes her *Ate* who tells Mitch about her past and destroys his illusion of her. Instead Mitch comes, drunk and vindictive,
to seduce Blanche. His mother-attachment blocks what might have
been a solution for him—Blanche now "isn't clean enough to bring
into the house with his mother." He tears the colored lamp shade off to
hold the naked bulb up into Blanche's haggard face. Unable to seduce
Blanche as he hoped, he leaves and Blanche packs in a state of shock,
deluding herself that she is going for a moonlight swim with spectral
gentleman callers. When Stella is rushed to the hospital in labor,
Blanche is left alone in the house with Stanley; if ever there were an
obligatory scene in the drama, this is it. Although she tries to defend
herself with a broken bottle, Stanley quickly disarms her and rapes
her, saying, "We've had this date with each other from the beginning."

When Stella comes home from the hospital with her baby, Blanche
is again having a hot bath, and has mentally withdrawn from reality.
She believes that an old gentleman caller whom she wrote is coming
to take her away. Stella and Stanley summon the doctor and nurse
from the state mental asylum, although Stella feels guilt over commit-
ing her sister and does not accept Blanche's story of Stan raping her.
Though she does Blanche a technical injustice, it cannot alter her
psychological destiny. Blanche is too psychotic now to be helped by the
Kowalskis, and has transferred all her life-hope from Mitch to the
illusionary gentleman caller whom she is sure will phone her. When
the doctor arrives, she seems aware at first that he is not the gentleman
caller, but when the doctor uses charm and gentleness instead of force,
Blanche goes off with him at the end humbly grateful for his solicitous
attention.

In *A Streetcar Named Desire,* Williams has depicted profoundly
the origins and growth of schizophrenia. He has shown Blanche struggling to master her conflicting drives of sex and *super-ego,* to live up
to an inner image of a belle of the old South while living in circumstances in which it is an anachronism. At first she is in rebellion against
her own nature but in touch with reality. As the various doors of
escape are closed to her and she finds Stanley across her one remaining
path, her mind is unable to cope with this impossible conflict. She
closes the door to reality and escapes to a psychotic world where
gallant gentlemen will give her shelter.

There were some critics who considered Blanche as fit only for a
hospital but not the tragic stage. Edward Chodorov, for example, ques-
tioned in his letter to the present author whether *Streetcar* met the
requirements of tragedy. The director of the Broadway production, Elia
Kazan, takes issue with Chodorov's position and in an astute analysis
calls the play a poetic tragedy:

We are shown the final dissolution of a person of worth, who once had great potential, and who, even as she goes down, has worth exceeding that of the 'healthy', coarse-grained figures who kill her.

It is not merely an academic issue to test a play such as *Streetcar* by the classic, Aristotelian standards, for with it much of the modern drama may stand or fall. As Kazan points out, Blanche is a character of some dignity who strives to rise above her circumstances. In the love scene with Mitch she lifts the play to universality, and Williams achieved the tragic irony of Sophocles in the discrepancy between reality and Blanche's distorted impression of it. Aristotelians balk, however, at the fact that Blanche achieves no insight, and to the contrary regresses until her final exit is made with no sublime tragic awareness of the forces that determined her destiny. But there is an escape from the dilemma—modern psychoanalytic psychology suggests a reinterpretation of Aristotle that restores *Streetcar* to the rank of tragic drama and at the same time confirms the universal insight of the observant Stagirite. It is simply that although Blanche closes her mind to any awareness as she escapes to psychosis, the insight happens *to the audience*. Williams is able to depict with his raw power the growth of psychosis out of simple defense mechanism, to show the conflict in a sensitive spirit between ugly reality and the quest for beauty. Blanche's tragedy is that of the individual unable to integrate the sex drive, to reconcile the physical hunger with tender and spiritual yearnings. Because of her sheltered background she cannot find security by other means than sexual ones. Thus she has as little free will to choose her destiny as had Oedipus. By illuminating Blanche's sickness, by dramatizing the dark unconscious forces with which Blanche grapples and by which she is defeated, the dramatist, like the psychoanalyst, makes it possible for others to be purged of guilt and fear, to say "There, but for the grace of whatever mental health I have been able to achieve, go I." To understand and participate in Blanche's fate is to escape it. Williams must be credited with a psychological masterpiece; *Streetcar* is powerful naturalism but also infinitely more—it affords a clear perception into the pressures that degrade, both the social forces which make for an environment of brutality and the individual's unconscious forces which make him a psychic cripple helpless to deal with his environment. Blanche is no less a tragic figure than Antigone or Medea—whether she is literally destroyed or whether it is only her mind seems but a technicality. It is a tragic experience in the theatre to participate in the disintegration of a personality.

The Southern Gentlewoman

by Signi Falk

In *A Streetcar Named Desire* the southern gentlewoman, the last representative of a dying culture, is too delicate to withstand the crudeness and decay surrounding her. The conflict between her standards and those represented by the primitive laborer finally destroy her. It is the study of this final descent into madness, with all its implied comment about the two codes, that seems to interest the playwright. It is characteristic of Williams, however, that he does not take a stand, for he romanticizes both the natural man and the decadent aristocrat.

Blanche Du Bois, the last relic of the decayed southern plantation, "Belle Rêve," enters the Vieux Carré section of New Orleans: her first line seems to give a clue to the theme of the play, that life is equated with passion, and its opposite is death. Actual trolley names provide Williams with appropriate symbols. Blanche was told to take a streetcar named Desire, transfer to one named Cemetaria, and get off at Elysian Fields—nomenclature that mixes Freud and classical mythology. It would take a Tennessee Williams to place the sex-happy adult children of the New Orleans slums in the Greek Isles of the Blessed. In this Gulf Coast heaven which lies between the river and the tracks, and where the "Blue Piano" in the bar around the corner symbolizes the easy mingling of Negro and white, there lives a colony of married couples whose lives represent sexual contentment, uninhibited and unashamed.

The entrance of Blanche, delicate as a moth and dressed in white— all of Williams' sexual deviates are dressed in immaculate white— and looking as if she were about to take cocktails or tea in the best drawing room or garden, is an incongruous and shocking intrusion. This is her first visit to her sister, Stella, who is married to a Polish– American mechanic, Stanley Kowalski; contented with her commonplace life, Stella is undisturbed by the vulgarities of her friends and neighbors. The contrast between the two sisters—Stella as the normal,

"The Southern Gentlewoman." From Chapter 3 in Signi Falk, Tennessee Williams, *Twayne's United States Authors Series* (New York, Twayne Publishers, Inc., 1962). *Reprinted by permission of the publishers.*

happy, and average woman; Blanche as the refined, hypersensitive, and decadent aristocrat—is soon obvious. It is also apparent that the arrival of this older sister, a representative of the civilized world and one most critical of the primitive mores of the Vieux Carré, will threaten the happy marital arrangement between Stella and Stan.

The explanation of Stella's happiness and willing descent to the cave apparently rests in the sexual charm of the man she married. Stan is a particularized characterization of the primitive hero who bears some similarity to the D. H. Lawrence type as exemplified by Mellors in *Lady Chatterley's Lover*—a type which Williams tentatively portrayed in Hadrian in *You Touched Me!* and partly in Val Xavier in *Battle of Angels*. The playwright's romantic ecstasy has a wistful note, for he indulges in a paean to virility that epitomizes the romantic admiration of the little man for the vigorous virility of a male hero. This deification of sex is the most enthusiastic passage in the whole canon of Tennessee Williams and is one statement which indicates where his heart is. Stan is the epitome of the pleasure an animal enjoys with his body, an aggressive, indulgent, powerful, and proud expression of sex. Williams describes him:

> *Animal joy in his being is implicit in all his movements and attitudes. Since earliest manhood the center of his life has been pleasure with women, the giving and taking of it, not with weak indulgence, dependently, but with the power and pride of a richly feathered male bird among hens. Branching out from this complete and satisfying center are all the auxiliary channels of his life, such as his heartiness with men, his appreciation of rough humor, his love of good drink and food and games, his car, his radio, everything that is his, that bears his emblem of the gaudy seed-bearer. He sizes up women with a glance, with sexual satisfactions, crude images flashing into his mind and determining the way he smiles at them.*

The clash between Blanche and Stan is inevitable, for they represent two opposite views of life. The play, however, is not a simple, clear-cut conflict between two equally strong forces but a subtle and sometimes rather confused study of character; rich in overtones, the play is sometimes weighted with significance implied rather than expressed. A play that has moments of greatness, it misses being great because the playwright had no clear idea of what he was trying to say. The complicated and rather contradictory characterization of Blanche, the failure to follow through and dramatize the conflict, and Williams' inability to resist writing "something wild" instead of extracting the fullest significance from his materials—all of these factors exhibit a weakness in the playwright's handling of the material.

The first clash between Blanche and Stanley arises over the loss of the plantation which he dreamed of owning. He suspects that she has

squandered the property. He yanks out of the trunk, which dominates
the kitchen, showy pieces of clothing and costume jewelry which he
thinks are expensive. When he touches a sheaf of papers, Blanche's
contempt is immediate; she says that the touch of his hands con-
taminates them. She gives the first hint of her private sorrow when
she identifies them as poems of a dead husband whom she hurt as
badly as Stan would hurt her. She says that she is protected because
she is no longer young and vulnerable. She vaguely suggests that the
plantation was lost on mortgages; she tells about family history which
is part of her heritage. In highly exaggerated language she tells how
the plantation was eaten away by spendthrift grandfathers and uncles
and father and brothers—Williams loves so much these exaggerations
—who over the years mortgaged the land to pay for their "epic fornications." Blanche's sexy by-play at the beginning of this scene rouses
Stan's suspicion about his sister-in-law and gives him an early clue for
his mode of revenge. The unsteadiness of her mind is suggested by the
way she flits from one subject or one feeling to another, always, however, coming back to her own delusions about herself.

The next clash occurs when Stella and Blanche return about two-
thirty in the morning to interrupt the men's poker game. The scenes
with Stan and his poker-playing pals, where the characterizations are
vivid and the dialogue a brilliant imitation of the idiom of an elemental people, are well handled. Williams makes an interesting
comment on the early writing of the play: "I settled for a while at
Chapala to work on a play called *The Poker Night* which later became
A Streetcar Named Desire." If the third scene was the beginning of the
play, then the southern gentlewoman theme must have been a later addition. The description of the poker scene, inspired by a Van Gogh
picture of a billiard parlor, is a good example of the way Williams uses
contrasting colors for dramatic effect. The scene calls to mind lines
which he gave to D. H. Lawrence in *I Rise in Flame, Cried the
Phoenix*; the British writer claimed for the artist the right to express
himself in violent colors. But though Williams notes especially that the
colors are those raw ones from childhood's spectrum, his characters
represent coarse men at their physical prime—men as powerful as
primary colors. Almost as if by habit Williams places together childhood innocence and sexual prowess. Part of the confusion in the play
arises not only from his glowingly wistful admiration for Stan and his
friends and for their capacity for unlimited physical pleasure, but also
from his sentimental support and sympathy for Blanche who degener-
ated pitifully with the same kind of physical indulgence.

In the poker scene a number of elements intrude in the inevitable
Blanche–Stan conflict. Blanche singles out Mitch as the one seemingly
respectable player and stops him on his way to "The Little Boy's

Room," as she calls it. She speaks pathetically of her great sorrow, of her need to cover up ugly truth—with a Williams' symbolic touch, she asks him to cover a naked light bulb with a paper Chinese lantern—and of the aesthetic problems of an English teacher working with "bobby soxers and drug-store Romeos." When she turns on the radio to encourage Mitch to dance, Stan in a drunken fury seizes the radio and hurls it out the window. He brutally strikes his wife, Stella, who tries to send the men home. In the brawl that follows, the women escape and the poker players soothe their violent companion. When he realizes that his wife is gone, Stan throws back his head and howls like a dog, yelling out her name. When she returns quietly, tears in her eyes, they rush together moaning like animals. He falls to his knees, presses his face against her delicately rounded belly, and she with tenderness raises him to her. He lifts her into his arms and carries her into the dark flat. The sight of this connubial bliss, following so closely upon the scene of drunken brutality, stuns Blanche for a moment. She soon, however, focuses her attention upon Mitch, the one unattached man who may offer the kindness that she needs.

The following morning Stella is serene and happy. Williams compares the tranquility on her face to the narcotic inner peace reflected on the images of Eastern idols—a very fancy way of glorifying pregnancy. It recalls his habitual way of equating sexual intercourse and religious rites. Stella explains to Blanche that the row wasn't serious, and she assures her sister that she is not in anything that she wants to get out of. Nevertheless, Blanche, living in her delusions, babbles on about telephoning an old beau, Shep Huntleigh, now a rich oil man and married, to plead for an escape. Blanche tries to impress upon Stella the depths to which she has sunk in her marriage, and unaware that Stan overhears her, she describes him as she sees him. She vents her contempt for a man who eats, moves, and talks like an animal— an interesting contrast to the playwright's paean describing Stan as a glorious male. Blanche calls him a sub-human, an ape, a survivor of the stone age bearing raw meat home to his mate, a throwback after thousands of years of civilization. She pleads melodramatically with her sister not to return to the brutes, but the plea is wasted on Stella who has a very different feeling about Stan. . . .

Stan avenges these continuing insults as he begins to confront Blanche with veiled questions about a man named Shaw, the hotel "Flamingo," and the town of Laurel. Stan has obviously struck a sore spot, for Blanche later explains herself to her sister in half-truths. Her sentimentally expressed lines anticipated the lurid confession which comes later. She explains that soft people have to seek the favor of hard ones, have to play a seductive role, be soft, resort to magic—to pay for a night's lodging. She explains that she's been running from one shelter to another trying to escape the storm, that she has depended on men's lovemaking to give her a sense of existence. To Stella, whose approach to sex is frank and simple, this talk is only morbid.

In spite of her pretty explanation, Blanche senses that her welcome is wearing thin and that her last refuge lies in marrying Mitch. Blanche—who flirted so indecently with Stan; who exhibited herself before the poker players; who called a strange young man collecting for papers a young Arabian prince and kissed him softly on the mouth —plays as prim and coy with Mitch as if she were sixteen and pure. At the same time, this southern gentlewoman sets the scene as if for a seduction—perhaps Williams' way of indicating that the lady is slightly confused. And then, a chance remark from Mitch about loneliness— there would seem to be more loneliness in the plays of Tennessee Williams than in all the lonely crowds of the entire United States—elicits her confession about her early marriage.

The boy she married, though not effeminate looking, had something different about him—a tenderness, an unmasculine softness, and nervousness. He had turned to her for help, she found out later, but she did not realize it. She describes him as struggling in quicksands and herself as slipping down with him. Then she found her husband with an older man in an unmistakable situation. Because of her expression of disgust, Allan shot himself. Blanche, desperate for a home, pours out this confession in a drunken, half-dazed condition. This recital is accompanied by sounds associated with the tragedy—a locomotive whistle and polka music—and suggests her present psychological state. Mitch takes her in his arms and she says, "Sometimes—there's God—so quickly!"

On a September afternoon Stan returns armed with revenge against the sister-in-law who called him sub-human. He reports to Stella that Blanche is not the modest white lily she pretends to be but a liar; that she was so famous at the "Flamingo Hotel" that she had to turn in her room key; that she was fired from her teaching job because she became involved with a seventeen-year-old boy. He also tells Stella that he has reported his findings to Mitch, a war-time buddy and his best friend, and that he has bought a return bus ticket for Blanche— to Laurel. All this information is reported to Stella who refuses to believe; she is remembering the older sister she knew as a child. It would seem that Williams threw away a naturally dramatic scene when he did not allow Stan to face Blanche directly with her lies. It represents the culmination of his revenge and the reason he has needed to clear his home of the unwelcome visitor. The scene could logically have precipitated the insanity which is evident in the closing scene.

Aware that disaster is closing in on her, Blanche tells the angry Mitch how much she needs him, and her deteriorating mental condition is conveyed by the polka music. In another confession scene she spills out the full hideous story of her degradation: her intimacies with strangers after her poet–husband's death, the affair with the seventeen-year-old boy, and her dismissal from her teaching job. She needs Mitch, she says, as a refuge from the world. She tells him of the endless acquaintances she has had with the dying. Then she adds another unsavory chapter to her biography: not far from the plantation was an army training camp. On Saturday nights the soldiers would return drunk from town, stagger across her lawn, call her name, and she would slip out to answer their calls. Later the paddy wagon collected the boys and returned them to the camp. Such a biographical account, even with the widest possible stretch of the imagination, hardly seems to belong to the delicate, moth-like, mentally unbalanced Blanche Du Bois.

Mary McCarthy wrote that Williams "is addicted to the embroider-ing lie" in his characterization of Blanche. "But the thin, sleazy stuff of this character must be embellished by Mr. Williams with all sorts of decorations. It is not enough that she should be a drunkard (this is in itself plausible); she must also be a notorious libertine who has been run out of a small town like a prostitute, a thing absolutely incon-ceivable for a woman to whom conventionality is the end of existence." In addition to her "interesting biography," which Miss McCarthy finds incredible, "she must be a symbol of art and beauty, this poor flimsy creature to whom truth is mortal, who hates the feel of experi-ence with a pathological aversion . . . she who has never spoken an honest word in her life is allowed, indeed encouraged, to present her life to the audience as a vocational decision, an artist's election of the beautiful, an act of supreme courage, the choice of the thorny way."

Mitch has the same ingenuousness as that other gentleman caller, Jim O'Connor. He talks of his heavy perspiration and of his fight against getting soft in the belly, but he has a code of honor and a diffidence about women that make him a little awed before the seem-ingly aristocratic Blanche. When he discovers what she really is, he is not so much shocked as hurt—the extent of her degeneracy seems not to have destroyed his love for her. Nevertheless, he reproaches her as not clean enough to present to his mother. As the bashful boy turned rake, he makes tentative advances to the prim prostitute who effects his speedy exit by yelling, "Fire!" It may be that Williams' real interest in the scene was in the symbolic, decorative elements—a blind Mexican woman peddling tin flowers, the kind displayed at funerals, and calling out in Spanish that she is selling flowers for the dead. It is against the old woman's mournful cries that Blanche insists that she never lied in her heart. Her legacy has been death, all the hideous, ugly manifestations of the dying that she faced alone. The opposite of death, she says, is desire. Richard Asselineau reported that during the time he was writing *Streetcar* Williams fancied that he had cancer and it was the good friendship of Carson McCullers that helped him to recover from his moribund imagination. He said that it is not surprising, therefore, that the play is so permeated with ideas of death.

Stan returns from the hospital to find a very much confused Blanche decked out in crumpled, white satin evening dress and shabby silver slippers, and wearing a rhinestone tiara on her head. In her drunken exhilaration she talks of a Caribbean cruise with her one-time sweetheart, now a millionaire; she plays the role of the aristocrat, the woman of intelligence, refinement, and beautiful spirit and refers to Stan and Mitch as swine. Angered by her superiority and pretensions, Stan flatly tells her that it is all lies, conceit, and tricks. He tells her to face the facts, to look at herself and her rag-picker outfit, and to recall that she may think of herself as a queen but she has been swilling his liquor. The speech gives an interesting contrast between the blunt realist who sees the powder and perfume and the paper lanterns over the light bulb for what they are and the romantic dreamer who lives in her imagination.

The rest of the scene is fever pitched. Blanche, like a cornered animal, makes desperate and pointless calls to Western Union. The state of Blanche's mind is pictorially suggested by the lurid reflections, grotesque and menacing shadows, that appear on the walls; the mood is intensified by off-stage noises symbolizing inhuman jungle cries. The excitement is heightened by offstage pantomime. Through the transparent back wall can be seen a portrayal of the struggle between a prostitute and a drunk, a scene interrupted by a policeman's whistle.

Stan emerges from the bedroom dressed in his silk wedding pajamas, grins at her deliberately, corners her. She tries to get away—in the background the "blue piano" begins pianissimo and increases to the roar of an approaching locomotive—erotic symbolism, perhaps, but a good stage trick. Stan moves stealthily toward her. Frantically she breaks a bottle and threatens to twist the broken end in his face. He springs toward her, snatches her wrist. Then come the beautifully loaded final lines of the scene: "Tiger—tiger! Drop that bottle-top! Drop it! We've had this date with each other from the beginning! (*She moans. The bottle-top falls. She sinks to her knees. He picks up her inert figure and carries her to the bed. The hot trumpet and drum from the Four Deuces sound loudly.*)" Perhaps this situation is the culmination of Stan's "revenge," or only an incident in Blanche's decline into insanity, or perhaps this is a necessary culmination of many "come-on" scenes Blanche has played, suggesting an equivalent to the old dramatic cliché of the long-delayed rape. One thing is certain. It makes brilliant use of all the old theatrical devices. It has the quality of a big finale, loud brass and full percussion. It also has that unmistakable, profitable, high-keyed, emotional box-office appeal.

In the final scene which occurs weeks later, Blanche, now obviously deranged, dresses to leave as if she were going to dinner with Shep Huntleigh. She immediately recognizes that the doctor is not the man from Dallas but, when he speaks softly to her and smiles, he is another suitor; she is won. The lurid reflections fade, the inhuman voices grow quiet. Clinging to his arm, she leaves quietly: "Whoever you are—I have always depended on the kindness of strangers." Broken by her excursion into Vieux Carré and its brutal realities, she escapes completely into her own mad world—and she ironically does so like an aristocrat.

Blanche in a number of ways resembles Amanda—her pretentions to gentility, her legend about her former suitors, and her habit of lying to herself and to others. But also, as with Laura, Williams has been overzealous in his explanation of her pitiable condition. Too many factors have contributed to her insanity. Her frequent references to death-bed responsibilities, her girlhood marriage to a poet–homosexual, the fear of poverty and loneliness, her frustrated need for love and companionship could explain her condition. But on the other side, the nymphomatic tendencies which she seems to have inherited, her almost pathological care of her body, her pretenses to virtue and her exhibitionism at the slightest excuse, and her eagerness to tell her whole lurid story—all these add up to something theatrical and deliberately sensational. As if that were not enough, she is the last aristocrat of an old order, an intellectual of sorts, something of a poet by nature, and the easy mark for the insensitive. As Mary McCarthy has implied, there is no wonder that confusion arises about the playwright's intentions.

The controversy that has stormed over Tennessee Williams can be very well illustrated by the widely different reactions to this play. The drama critics recognized a distinctive talent, were intrigued by the scope and the complexity of the play, but were disturbed by the ambiguities and the pretensions. Brooks Atkinson in his review of the stage production found the play "almost unbearably tragic." The audience, he reported, came away "profoundly moved. . . . For they have been sitting all evening in the presence of truth, and that is a rare and wonderful experience." Without flatly stating that Blanche is closer to the theater than to life, he kindly said: "Since she is created on the stage as a distinct individual, experiences identical with hers can never be repeated. She and the play that is woven about her are unique." Joseph Wood Krutch stated that, in spite of the sensational quality of the story, "the author's perceptions remain subtle and delicate and he is amazingly aware of nuances even in situations

where nuance might seem to be inevitably obliterated by violence."
He believed Williams' stories "enable him to communicate emotions
which have special, personal significance," so that it can be taken
for granted that "his plays will be immediately recognizable by their
familiar themes and a sensibility as unique as that of a lyric poet."

A Streetcar Named Desire won two major awards and became big
business. A two-year run on Broadway and road-company productions
for approximately three and a half million American theatergoers—
and packed houses in London, Rome, Stockholm, Copenhagen, and
Mexico City—afford solid proof that Tennessee Williams can reach
a wide and varied audience. It became one of the best-known plays
in the mid-twentieth-century American repertory, partly because of
its originality, but also because of the heated arguments over morality
and art that it aroused.

Tennessee Williams:
Streetcar to Glory

by C. W. E. Bigsby

The theatre has long been the poor relation of the American arts and Eugene O'Neill's Nobel Prize (like Sinclair Lewis's and Pearl Buck's) was a gesture having more political than cultural significance. For all the interest of Kingsley, Odets and Hellman, indeed, American drama is largely a post-war phenomenon and its new and enhanced prestige owes a great deal to a man who started his working life in a warehouse, writing poems on shoe boxes.

Thomas Lanier Williams was born on March 26, 1914. His parents were a travelling salesman and the daughter of the local minister—which may account for the strange mixture of prurience and puritanism in his work. His first play was written in 1935 and he scored a moderate local success in St. Louis with a series of plays written for a little theatre group called *The Mummers*.

The forties, however, opened somewhat inauspiciously. His first play intended for Broadway production, *Battle of Angels*, was withdrawn after its Boston try-out. Nevertheless in the course of the following two decades he emerged as a major dramatist and attained the two-fold distinction of being awarded a Pulitzer Prize and being banned from the public stage in Britain, surviving both experiences reasonably intact. Always controversial, his plays were welcomed not only for their unique vision but also for the frankness and vitality which they brought to a theatre all too often starved of those qualities.

Critics have often been at pains to draw a distinction between Tennessee Williams and Arthur Miller on the basis that the former is concerned with personal fears and frustrations while the latter is concerned with social issues. Yet Williams, too, has his roots in the social theatre of the 30's while, like Miller's *All My Sons* and *Death of a Salesman*, most of his work is concerned with the plight of the

"*Tennessee Williams: Streetcar to Glory*" by C. W. E. Bigsby. *Excerpted from* The Forties: Fiction, Poetry, Drama (*Deland, Fla.: Everett/Edwards, Inc., 1969*). *Reprinted by permission of Everett/Edwards and Warren French.*

individual in the modern world. *The Mummers* itself was a radical group and the plays which he produced for it were largely protest dramas.

The atmosphere of hysteria and violence in his work is, therefore, not merely an expression of personal neurosis. It is also a legacy which he has inherited from a theatre in which emotionalism, sentimentality and violent action were seen as legitimate substitutes for dramatic tension. Like Miller, too, he has inherited not merely the over-simplifications of agit-prop drama but also a suspicion of wealth itself. In common with Brick, in *Cat on a Hot Tin Roof,* he is in fact something of an "ass aching Puritan." Thus the division between rich and poor in his work is, for the most part, also a division between brutality and compassion, sterility and vitality. He is enough of an old-fashioned moralist, indeed, to see bodily disease as the fruit of sin. Thus the rich are frequently pictured as being eaten away from within: Boss Finley (*Sweet Bird of Youth*) apparently by tuberculosis, his daughter by syphilis, Mrs. Venable (*Suddenly Last Summer*) by madness, Jabe Torrence (*Orpheus Descending*) and even the rich but attractive Big Daddy (*Cat on a Hot Tin Roof*) by cancer. Perhaps this is why Williams, a man who sold the film rights of one of his plays for half a million dollars, is so concerned about his own health.

On the other side of the coin are the pure in heart; the poets, romantics, bohemians, and, of course, playwrights. For he has hardly written a single play which is not obliquely concerned with his own plight as a writer in a world which values only material things. When Cervantes was asked whom he intended to represent through the figure of Don Quixote he is said to have replied, "Myself." Williams might well give the same reply with regard to any of a dozen characters. So it is that in the persons of Laura Wingfield, Blanche DuBois, Alma Winemiller, we have a series of portraits of those characters for whom Williams has the greatest sympathy; those who, like himself, have been unable fully to adjust to a world in which honor, sexual passion, integrity and compassion no longer have a place.

Williams' first Broadway success came with *The Glass Menagerie* in 1945. This play, which won the New York Drama Critics' Award, exhibits a delicacy and control frequently lacking from his later work. . . .

Obviously the play has a special meaning for the playwright who had himself lived the nightmare which he describes but it also functions as an image of the world as Williams sees it. For he has said that "for me the dominating premise has always been the need for understanding and tenderness and fortitude among individuals trapped by circumstances." Clearly the play's setting—"the Wingfield apartment is . . . one of those vast hive-like conglomerations of cellular living units"—is, therefore, concerned with emphasizing not merely the physical oppressiveness of life lived in a materialistic society but also the destruction of the human spirit which seems, to Williams, a natural corollary of modern living.

Moreover Laura herself is not merely a disturbingly accurate picture of his own sister. She stands also as an image of Williams' central theme; the destructive impact of society on the sensitive individual. . . . Looking for compassion she is brought face to face with the brutality of a world in which there is an apparently unbridgeable gulf between aspiration and fulfillment. This is a lesson, too, which has to be learnt both by Blanche DuBois, in Williams' second Broadway success of the 40's, *A Streetcar Named Desire,* and by Alma Winemiller, in *Summer and Smoke,* written before *Streetcar* but not performed until the following year.

Williams' world, for the most part, has the simplicity and directness of moral allegory. Good is opposed to evil, spirituality to sensuality and the romantic to the brutally realistic. Indeed his characters are all too often simply manipulated in order to fulfill their functional roles in his modern parables. . . . Yet with his next play, *Streetcar,* which won both the New York Drama Critics' Award and the Pulitzer Prize, he showed that he was fully alive to the complexity of human nature and to the danger of facile moralising.

The mood of *A Streetcar Named Desire* is effectively summed up by the opening paragraph of a book which Williams greatly admired, *Lady Chatterley's Lover.* Here Lawrence had expressed his view of man's situation in the modern world: "Ours is essentially a tragic age, so we refuse to take it tragically. The cataclysm has happened, we are among the ruins, we start to build up new little habitats, to have new little hopes. It is rather hard work: there is now no smooth road into the future: but we go round or scramble over the obstacles. We've got to live, no matter how many skies have fallen." Williams' play is concerned with just such an attempt to discover a means and a purpose for life in surroundings which seem to offer little grounds for hope. As one of the characters says, "Life has got to go on. No matter what happens, you've got to keep on going."

Lawrence's influence on Williams has been plotted before but is especially important with regard to the work which he produced during the 40's and to *Streetcar* in particular. In 1939 he had gone to Taos, New Mexico, to interview Frieda Lawrence. He had long been planning a play about Lawrence's death and this now finally took some kind of shape. Significantly he described the theme of this play, *I Rise in Flame, Cried the Phoenix,* as "a man's . . . pilgrimage through times inimical to human beings." As such it clearly anticipates not only *Streetcar* but also much of Williams' later work. In 1945 he once again turned to Lawrence, this time adapting one of his short stories but it was not until *Streetcar* that he managed fully to digest his Lawrentian lessons and incorporate them into his own per- ception of an America caught in transition from genteel sterility to brutal indifference.

Blanche DuBois is a thirty-year-old woman who, when young, had made a disastrous marriage. Her husband had turned out to be a homosexual and in forcing him to face this fact she had provoked his suicide. Unable to admit to what she had done or to accept the lone- liness which stretches out ahead of her, she turns, like Alma in *Sum- mer and Smoke,* to a series of casual intimacies with strangers and is finally run out of town when she seduces a sixteen year old boy.

At the beginning of the play she arrives in New Orleans to stay with her sister, Stella, fully aware that she no longer has anywhere else to run. The two sisters had been brought up on a Southern plan- tation but Stella has abandoned the aristocratic pretensions to which Blanche clings so desperately. She has married Stanley Kowalsky, a Polish immigrant worker, and, much to Blanche's disgust, appears to revel both in her husband's brutality and his sensuality.

Hope suddenly appears for Blanche, however, in the person of Mitch, a lumbering mother's boy. He is attracted to her and she realizes that marriage will provide a kind of answer to her problems. But she reckons without Stanley. There is an instinctual animosity between these two. Blanche responds to him with a pathetic mixture of aristocratic contempt and unsubtle flirtation, while Stanley sees in her only a threat to his own way of life. When he discovers the truth about her past, therefore, he warns Mitch off and completes her de- struction by raping her as his own wife is in a hospital having his baby. The play ends as Blanche, now mentally unhinged, is led away from the apartment by a doctor and nurse, her contact with reality finally severed.

We are offered, it seems, a hopeless choice between decadence and brutality and, like Williams himself, have to pick our way through the personal treacheries and frustrations in an attempt to find some- thing worthwhile endorsing. For if Williams rebels against the cruelty of the modern age he clearly recognizes too the irrelevance of Blanche's posturing. Yet for all that, she—and the Southern tradition which she represents—obviously holds an attraction for Williams which goes beyond a romantic regret for past glory. He values the Southern past, in fact, not because he has any illusions as to the nature of its justice or the quality of its life but simply because, to his mind, it represents order. Here the anarchic power of sexuality was masked behind a cultivated manner and the naked pursuit of wealth cloaked by the

whole cavalier tradition of the South. Like Joseph Conrad he felt that
we are saved from chaos only by the "sovereign power enthroned in
a fixed standard of conduct." The ordered nature of society in turn
suggested a cosmic order and purpose. Now, in the modern age, the
veneer has been stripped away and the structure of society has dis-
integrated. The individual is forced to admit to the reality of flux,
to what one of Williams' characters describes as "the terrible—fast—
dark—rush of events." It is this new, impersonal, world "sick with
neon," which terrifies Williams and his protagonists. For, with order
destroyed, the individual falls victim to what he sees as the blind
illogic of much of human activity.

Williams' personal reaction is the predictable response of the artist.
By the act of writing he tries to re-impose a sense of order. The creative act itself thus becomes an act of defiance, or, in another light,
a form of escapism. This, indeed, is how one of his characters, significantly called simply, The Writer, justifies himself in a one act play
called "The Lady of Larkspur Lotion"—a play which in many ways
anticipates *Streetcar*: "Suppose that I, to make this nightmare bear-
able for as long as I must continue to be the helpless protagonist of
it—suppose that I ornament, illuminate—glorify it! With dreams and
fancies! . . . suppose that I live in this world of pitiful fiction! What
satisfaction can it give [anyone] to tear it to pieces, to crush it—call
it a *lie*? . . . There are no lies but the lies that are stuffed in the
mouth by the hard knuckled hand of need, the cold fist of necessity."
The same is true of his other protagonists. Some, like Tom Wingfield,
Sebastian Venable, and Chris Flanders, are writers themselves; others,
like Laura Wingfield, Alma Winemiller and Blanche DuBois, are
simply content to retreat into a world of illusion. Blanche, for example, invents a lover who will come and rescue her and by an act of
will transforms her harsh surroundings, placing a paper lantern over
the electric light and filling the place with pastel shades. But the
final futility of this response is amply demonstrated in *Streetcar* when
Blanche's desperate pretence is shattered by a man "as coarse and
direct and powerful as the primary colors." For illusion is only effective so long as others are prepared to tolerate it. Hence there is a
sad truth to the popular song which Blanche sings as a counterpoint
to Stanley's revelations of her debauchery: "It's a Barnum and Bailey
world. Just as phony as it can be. But it wouldn't be make believe
if you believed in me."

The real hero of the play, therefore, is Stella, for she alone is prepared to offer the necessary comfort and understanding. Like Connie
Chatterley she discovers a genuine fulfillment based on sexuality but,
more significantly, she thereby stumbles on the urgent need for that
tenderness and compassion which, to both Williams and Lawrence,

is the key to the human predicament. If she emerges also as the weakest character in the play this is because, however much he feels committed to seeking out some positive response to the modern world, Williams' sympathies are always with the weak and defeated while his admiration is always with those who manage to survive in and even dominate contemporary society. These latter—men like John Buchanan and Stanley Kowalsky—are described by Williams as Promethean figures "brilliantly alive in a stagnant society." Yet for all their vitality these "Prometheans" are too much a product of the modern world to offer any real hope. John Buchanan, before his somewhat incredible *volte face*, lacks true compassion and sympathy while Stanley Kowalsky's brutality towards Blanche finally disqualifies his mindless sensuality as a viable alternative. Nevertheless, despite this inhumanity there are moments of tenderness between Stella and Stanley which clearly offer some slight hope for the future. For Williams, in surveying the post-war world, has said that "the only satisfactory thing we are left with in this life is the relations—if they're sincere—between people," love being "the closest we've come" to such a satisfying relationship. Where the modern European theatre stresses the impossibility of communication he continues to insist that some kind of contact is possible. But like Arthur Miller, in *After the Fall,* he is prepared to confess that this contact is imperfect and the love which it engenders an incomplete answer to the human condition. This, indeed, is the sense of the Hart Crane poem which Williams uses as an epigraph to *Streetcar.* For this is a poem which describes not only the desperate situation of Blanche DuBois and her fellow romantics but also the plight of a dramatist who from *Battle of Angels* onwards committed himself to a cause which perhaps seemed lost from the very beginning:

> And so it was that I entered the broken world
> To trace the visionary company of love, its voice
> An instant in the wind (I know not whither hurled)
> But not for long to hold each desperate choice.

Chronology of Important Dates

(*Note:* The life of Tennessee Williams was never front-page news in any sense of the word, although his plays, of course, were nearly always headline material. The following dates reflect important points in Williams' life up to the production of *A Streetcar Named Desire*. Thereafter, no attempt has been made to follow the playwright's wanderings around the globe.)

	Williams	*The Age*
1911	March 26: Born in Columbus, Miss.	
1918	July: Idyllic rural Southern childhood in Mississippi and Tennessee ends with move to St. Louis	World War I ends
1919	January: Birth of brother Dakin. Williams spends year with grandparents in Clarksburg, Miss.; beginning to read Dickens, Scott, Shakespeare	
1920		Election of Harding; return to "normalcy"
1923		Death of Harding; beginning of "Coolidge prosperity"
1927	April: $5.00 check from *Smart Set* magazine for first published item, "Can a Good Wife Be a Good Sport?"	
1928	June: $35.00 check from *Weird Tales* for "The Vengeance of Nitocris"	Election of Hoover

1929	September: Enters University of Missouri	Stock market crash; beginning of the Great Depression
1931	Removed from college in senior year by irate father for failing ROTC. Put to work at International Shoe Co.; writes endlessly at home at night	
1932		Election of Roosevelt
1935	March: Physical breakdown sends Williams to Memphis for year with grandparents. July 12: First production of a play, *Cairo! Shanghai! Bombay!* by Memphis Garden Players	
1936	September: Enters Washington University, St. Louis. Webster Groves Theatre Guild and The Mummers produce several Williams plays	
1937	September: Enters University of Iowa, awarded A.B. following spring Prefrontal lobotomy performed on Rose	
1938	Lives in New Orleans French Quarter	
1939	Summer: $100 prize from Group Theatre for *American Blues* awarded while living in southern California. December: $1,000 Rockefeller grant	Beginning of World War II
1940	Dec. 30: Opening and collapse of *Battle of Angels* in Boston	Fall of France; Battle of Britain
1941	First of four unsuccessful operations to remove cataract from left eye. Beginning of about three years of wandering in Georgia, Florida, New Orleans, New York, Washington, D.C., California	Pearl Harbor

1944	Dec. 26: Chicago opening of *The Glass Menagerie*	Invasion of Normandy
1945	March 31: New York opening of *Menagerie*. Wins New York Critics' Circle Award	Hiroshima; End of World War II
1947	Dec. 3: Opening of *A Streetcar Named Desire*. Wins second Critics' Prize and Pulitzer Prize. Williams' parents separate permanently	
1948		Election of Truman; Berlin blockade
1950		Beginning of Korean War
1952		Election of Eisenhower
1955	March 24: Opening of *Cat on a Hot Tin Roof*. Third Critics' Prize, second Pulitzer Prize Death of grandfather Walter E. Dakin at age ninety-eight	
1957	Death of father Cornelius Coffin Williams. After failure of *Orpheus Descending* (revision of *Battle of Angels*), enters year of psychoanalysis in attempt to overcome mounting fears and panic. Williams termed treatment unsuccessful	
1960		Election of Kennedy
1961	Dec. 28: Opening of *Night of the Iguana*. Wins fourth Critics' Prize	
1962	July: Failure of first of several versions of *The Milk Train Doesn't Stop Here Any More* in Spoleto, Italy	
1963		Assassination of Kennedy

1968   March: Failure of *The Seven*   Election of Nixon
            Descents of Myrtle

1969   January: Williams converted   First man on the moon
            to Roman Catholicism
            May: Failure of *In the Bar of a*
            Tokyo Hotel

Notes on the Editor and Contributors

JORDAN Y. MILLER, Chairman of the Department of English at the University of Rhode Island, has contributed several articles on American drama to various critical anthologies and periodicals. He is the author of *American Dramatic Literature, Eugene O'Neill and the American Critic,* and *Playwright's Progress: O'Neill and the Critics.*

BROOKS ATKINSON began as drama critic of the New York *Times* in 1925, and by the time of his retirement in 1960 was regarded as the "Dean" of newspaper critics, without whose praise, tradition held, a play could not possibly succeed. He is the author of many books and essays on the drama and the Broadway theatre.

HOWARD BARNES was drama critic for the New York *Herald-Tribune* during the 1940s, only slightly below the critical prestige of Atkinson and the *Times.*

CHRISTOPHER W. E. BIGSBY is one of the more important younger British scholars with serious interest in American drama. He attended graduate school in the United States under a Fulbright fellowship in 1963–64, and is now on the faculty of the University of East Anglia in Norwich, England. He has written several important books on American drama, including a full-length study of Edward Albee.

JOHN MASON BROWN was one of the foremost critics of American drama before and after the last war. His column of dramatic criticism, "Seeing Things," appeared in *The Saturday Review* for more than a decade until 1955. He served as drama critic on *Theatre Arts* as early as 1924, followed by the New York *Post* and the *World Telegram.* He published a score or more books of dramatic criticism.

JOHN CHAPMAN has been associated with the New York Daily *News* since 1920, serving as drama critic from 1943. He edited the Burns Mantle *Best Plays* series from 1947–52.

DURANT DA PONTE, widely recognized as a literary critic, was a member of the University of Tennessee Department of English and Assistant Dean of the Graduate School until his death in the mid-1960s.

SIGNI FALK, member of the English Department of Coe College, wrote one of the first book-length studies of Williams for the Twayne American Authors Series in 1961.

HAROLD HOBSON has served as critic for the *Christian Science Monitor* since 1933, and was drama critic for the London *Sunday Times* from 1944–49. He is the author of several critical books.

ELINOR HUGHES began her career as drama critic for the Boston *Herald* in 1935, covering many of the road show tryouts of O'Neill, Williams, and other major American playwrights.

ELIA KAZAN was a successful young actor and director in Harold Clurman's Group Theatre in the 1930s, making his reputation as a major director with the 1942 production of *The Skin of Our Teeth*. *Streetcar* was his first Williams play, followed by *Camino Real*, *Cat on a Hot Tin Roof*, *Sweet Bird of Youth*, and the motion picture versions of *Streetcar* and *Baby Doll*. Through a series of misunderstandings the long association with Williams ended in 1960.

JOSEPH WOOD KRUTCH served as drama critic for *The Nation* from 1924–59, and was Brander Matthews Professor of Drama at Columbia University from 1943–52. His *American Drama Since 1918* is one of the finest general histories, and his books such as *The Modern Temper* and *Modernism in Modern Drama* are important volumes.

RENÉ MACCOLL, critic for the *Atlantic Monthly*, served as overseas correspondent for that magazine during the 1950s.

MARION MAGID, in addition to regular critical contributions to the respected Jewish monthly, *Commentary*, writes dramatic criticism for several scholarly publications.

GEORGE JEAN NATHAN, through his outspoken distinctively biting style, exerted considerable influence on the developing American drama between wars. He was an ardent champion of Eugene O'Neill long before the playwright was widely known. Nathan began as drama critic on the New York *Herald* in 1905 and wrote or edited scores of books on the Broadway scene.

JOSEPH N. RIDDELL, Professor of English at Duke University, has been a large contributor to many journals in the field of American letters.

IRWIN SHAW wrote the most outstanding American anti-war play, *Bury the Dead*, in 1936. He was drama critic for the *New Republic* in 1947, and has written many radio serials, novels, and short stories, one of the most famous of which is *The Young Lions*.

W. DAVID SIEVERS was a classmate of Williams in the Dramatic Workshop of the New School for Social Research in the early 1940s. He was Professor of Theatre Arts at Long Beach, Calif., State College, and had associated during his lifetime with many active drama luminaries.

JOHN VON SZELISKI, literary critic and scholar, is Chairman of the Department of Drama at Williams College.

RICHARD WATTS, JR., is still active as drama critic of the New York *Post*. He has reviewed opening nights of major American plays for the *Post* and other New York newspapers since the 1920s.

PHILIP WEISSMAN is practicing psychologist and editor of the psychological journal, *American Imago*. His 1965 book, *Creativity in the Theatre,* is a lengthy study of psychoanalytic aspects of the drama.

Selected Bibliography

The items listed below comprise a highly selected list which, when used in conjunction with this volume, will provide a variety of biographical information about Williams as man and artist as well as further criticism of *A Streetcar Named Desire*. A comprehensive bibliography was published in *Modern Drama*, 1 (December 1958): 181–91, followed by a supplement in 2 (December 1959): 220–23.

Books

Donahue, Francis. *The Dramatic World of Tennessee Williams*. New York, Frederick Ungar Publishing Co., 1964.

A play-by-play review of Williams' output, with fairly extensive plot résumés. Some inaccuracies in the opening biographical chapter.

Falk, Signi Lenea. *Tennessee Williams*. New York, Twayne Publishers, Inc., 1962.

This contribution to Twayne's American Authors series is generally competent but contains glaring errors of date in its five-page chronology.

Fedder, Norman J. *The Influence of D. H. Lawrence on Tennessee Williams*. The Hague, Mouton & Co., 1966.

A slim volume outlining many of Lawrence's well-known influences on Williams' plays and stories

Hurrell, John D. *Two Modern American Tragedies*. New York, Charles Scribner's Sons, 1961.

This paperback research casebook has a very good collection of critical articles about Miller and Williams and their most famous tragedies, *Death of a Salesman* and *Streetcar*.

Jackson, Esther Merle. *The Broken World of Tennessee Williams*. Madison and Milwaukee, The University of Wisconsin Press, 1965.

A fairly comprehensive critical approach to the plays in view of Williams' own world outlook and the theater of his time.

Maxwell, Gilbert. *Tennessee Williams and Friends.* Cleveland and New York,
The World Publishing Company, 1965.

Williams seen through the eyes of a close personal friend and companion
in his leaner years.

Nelson, Benjamin. *Tennessee Williams: The Man and His Work.* New York,
Ivan Obolensky, Inc., 1961.

Straightforward biographical and critical summary of Williams' career.

Williams, Edwina Dakin, as told to Lucy Freeman. *Remember Me to Tom.*
New York, G. P. Putnam's Sons, 1963.

Highly personal, very readable, sometimes revealing account of Williams
and his family as related by his mother. Some excellent photographs of
parents and children at various ages.

Articles

Brooks, Charles B. "The Comic Tennessee Williams." *Quarterly Journal of
Speech,* 44 (October 1958): 275–81.

One of few scholarly discussions of Williams' ability as comic writer.
Streetcar discussed with other of his major works.

Callahan, Edward F. "Tennessee Williams' Two Worlds." *North Dakota
Quarterly,* 25 (Summer 1957): 61–67.

Streetcar, Summer and Smoke, Rose Tatoo, and *Glass Menagerie* are
treated as a tetralogy involving the analysis of modern man "wandering
between two worlds, one dead, the other powerless to be born."

Casty, Alan. "Tennessee Williams and the Small Hands of Rain." *Mad River
Review,* 1 (Fall–Winter 1965): 27–43.

A line by e. e. cummings, "nobody, not even the rain, has such small
hands," used as basis of discussion of the outer personal and inner sexual
struggles of Williams' characters.

Clurman, Harold. "A Streetcar Named Desire," in *Lies Like Truth* (New
York, The Macmillan Co., 1958), pp. 72–80. Reprinted in Hurrell, above.

Discussion of the play's effect and some of the critical reaction to it mainly
in terms of the acting.

Falk, Signi. "The Profitable World of Tennessee Williams." *Modern Drama,*
1 (December 1958): 172–80. Reprinted in Hurrell, above.

Review of certain character types common to Williams; particular emphasis on Blanche and Stanley.

Funatsu, Tatsumi. "Blanche's Loneliness in *A Streetcar Named Desire.*"
Kyushu American Literature, Kyushu Univ., Fukuoka City, Japan, No. 5
(April 1962): 36–41.

Interesting mainly because of the scholarly attention given Williams in this Japanese quarterly devoted to the study of American literature.

Ganz, Arthur. "The Desperate Morality of the Plays of Tennessee Williams." *American Scholar,* 31 (Spring 1962): 278–94.

While *Streetcar* receives comparatively limited treatment, this essay is unusual in its approach to Williams as a consistent, if unique, moralist.

Gibbs, Wolcott. "Lower Depths, Southern Style." *The New Yorker,* 23 (Dec. 13, 1947): 50–54.

After a fairly complete review of the plot, Gibb's moderate reaction to the play concludes that Williams does not need this "pseudo-poetic" decoration to hide lack of thought.

Jackson, Esther M. "Music and Dance as Elements of Form in the Drama of Tennessee Williams." *Révue d'histoire du théâtre,* Année 15, No. 3, (July–September 1963): 294–301.

Review of Williams' use of music and dance in *Streetcar* and other plays as a part of the attempt of modern drama to recover the "total theatre" of the ancients.

Jones, Robert Emmet. "Tennessee Williams' Early Heroines." *Modern Drama,* 2 (December 1959): 211–19. Reprinted in Hurrell, above.

Discussion of heroines from *Battle of Angels* through *Rose Tattoo* in terms of Williams' two types: relics of moribund gentility and examples of uncultured sensuality.

Kernan, Alvin B. "Truth and Dramatic Mode in the Modern Theatre: Chekhov, Pirandello, and Williams." *Modern Drama,* 1 (September 1958): 101–14.

The Seagull, Six Characters, and *Streetcar* discussed in terms of their approach to "reality" and "truth."

Lewis, Theophilus. "Freud and the Split-Level Drama." *Catholic World,* 187 (May 1958): 98–103.

Streetcar considered in an exploration of Freudian influences on drama that force the audience to grasp "two levels of intention, the apparent and the latent."

McCarthy, Mary. "A Streetcar Called Success," in *Sights and Spectacles.* New York, Farrar, Straus and Cudahy, 1956, pp. 131–35. Reprinted in author's *Theatre Chronicles,* New York, Farrar, Straus and Company, 1963.

A strong indictment of Williams' themes and motifs that make his work "reek of literary ambition" and "smell of careerism."

Popkin, Harry. "The Plays of Tennessee Williams." *Tulane Drama Review,* 4 (March 1960): 45–64.

Streetcar and other Williams plays shown to develop an archetypal pattern involving the healthy, handsome man (Adonis) and the older woman losing her looks (Gargoyle).

Taylor, Harry. "The Dilemma of Tennessee Williams." *Masses and Mainstream,* 1 (April 1948): 51–56. Reprinted in Hurrell, above.

Extended discussion of some of the problems Williams creates for himself in the artistic style he has chosen.